EDITING EARLY ENGLISH DRAMA:
SPECIAL PROBLEMS AND NEW DIRECTIONS

Previous Conference Publications

1965 *Editing Sixteenth-Century Texts*, ed. R.J. Schoeck (1966)

1966 *Editing Nineteenth-Century Texts*, ed. John M. Robson (1967)

1967 *Editing Eighteenth-Century Texts*, ed. D.I.B. Smith (1968)

1968 *Editor, Author, and Publisher*, ed. William J. Howard (1969)

1969 *Editing Twentieth-Century Texts*, ed. Francess G. Halpenny (1972)

1970 *Editing Seventeenth-Century Prose*, ed. D.I.B. Smith (1972)

1971 *Editing Texts of the Romantic Period*, ed. John D. Baird (1972)

1972 *Editing Canadian Texts*, ed. Francess G. Halpenny (1975)

1973 *Editing Eighteenth-Century Novels*, ed. G.E. Bentley, Jr. (1975)

1974 *Editing British and American Literature, 1880–1920*, ed. Eric W. Domville (1976)

1975 *Editing Renaissance Dramatic Texts: English, Italian, and Spanish*, ed. Anne Lancashire (1976)

1976 *Editing Medieval Texts: English, French, and Latin Written in England*, ed. A.G. Rigg (1977)

1977 *Editing Nineteenth-Century Fiction*, ed. Jane Millgate (1978)

1978 *Editing Correspondence*, ed. J.A. Dainard (1979)

1979 *Editing Illustrated Books*, ed. William Blissett (1980)

1980 *Editing Poetry from Spenser to Dryden*, ed. A.H. de Quehen (1981)

1981 *Editing Texts in the History of Science and Medicine*, ed. Trevor H. Levere (1982)

1982 *Editing Polymaths: Erasmus to Russell*, ed. H.J. Jackson (1983)

EDITING EARLY ENGLISH DRAMA: SPECIAL PROBLEMS AND NEW DIRECTIONS

Papers given at the nineteenth annual
Conference on Editorial Problems
University of Toronto
4–5 November 1983

EDITED BY

A.F. JOHNSTON

AMS PRESS, INC.
New York

Library of Congress Cataloging-in-Publication Data

Conference on Editorial Problems (19th : 1983 : University of Toronto)
  Editing early English drama, special problems and new directions.

  1. English drama—To 1500—Criticism, Textual—Congresses.   2. Mysteries and miracle-plays, English—Criticism, Textual—Congresses.   3. Moralities, English—criticism, Textual—Congresses.   4. Manuscripts, English (Middle)—Editing—Congresses.   5. Theater—England—history—Medieval, 500–1500—Congresses.
I. Johnston, Alexandra F., 1939–   . II. Title.
PR641.C66   1987   822'.1'09   86-28680
ISBN 0-404-63669-1

Copyright © 1987 by AMS Press, Inc.
All rights reserved

Published by
AMS Press, Inc.
56 East 13th Street
New York, N. Y. 10003

MANUFACTURED IN THE UNITED STATES OF AMERICA

Contents

Notes on Contributors	7
Introduction A.F. Johnston	13
Drama Editing and Its Relation to Recent Trends in Literary Criticism David Bevington	17
A Margin of Error: The Problems of Marginalia in *The Castle of Perseverance* David Parry	33
Stage Directions and the Editing of Early English Drama Peter Meredith	65
"this hawthorn-brake our tiring-house": Records of Early English Drama and Modern Play-texts. J.A.B. Somerset	95
The *York Cycle* and the *Chester Cycle*: What do the records tell us? Alexandra F. Johnston	121

Notes on Contributors

David Bevington is professor of English at the University of Chicago and editor of *Medieval Drama* and the Riverside edition of *The Collected Works of William Shakespeare*. His influential book *From Mankind to Marlowe* was one of the first fruits of the new critical approach to early drama twenty years ago. One of the leading scholars in North American early drama studies, he is the co-founder and chairman of the Medieval and Renaissance Drama section of the Modern Language Association and one of the members of the Advisory Board of Records of Early English Drama.

David Parry is the Theatrical Administrator of the *Poculi Ludique Societas* in Toronto. After a varied life in the practical end of the theatre in England and elsewhere, he entered the University of Hull as a mature student. He received his M.A. from the University of Victoria, and came to Toronto for his doctoral work in 1975. Since then he has been closely associated with the PLS and instrumental in the four major productions of the *York Cycle* in 1977, the *Castle of Perseverance* in 1979, the *N–Town Passion Play* in 1981 and the *Chester Cycle* in 1983. His doctoral dissertation grew from the production of *The Castle*. During 1983–84 he was a post-doctoral fellow at Cambridge University.

Peter Meredith is Senior Lecturer at the University of Leeds. One of the founding members of Records of Early English Drama and, since its inception, the British representative on the REED executive, he has been at the centre of new early drama scholarship in England for the last decade. He has been deeply involved in the *Leeds Texts and Monographs* Medieval Drama Facsimile Series and is co-founder and co-editor of *Medieval English Theatre*. He has been active in the productions of *York, Towneley* and *Chester* in England since 1975. Like David Parry, he brings the actor's eye to his scholarship.

J.A.B. Somerset is a professor of English at the University of Western Ontario. His early interest is reflected in his edition of *Four Tudor Interludes*, but more recently his editorial skills have been directed towards editing the records of Shropshire and Staffordshire for Records of Early English Drama. He is a member of the REED executive and the editor of a related series, Studies in Early English Drama, from the University of Toronto Press. He has recently undertaken a project involving the archives of the Stratford Festival of Canada.

Alexandra F. Johnston is professor of English at the University of Toronto and principal of Victoria College. She is the General Editor of Records of Early English Drama. She edited the first collection of records for the series, the *York Records*, with Dr. Margaret Rogerson and is now completing editions of the records of Berkshire and Buckinghamshire for REED.

She has been involved, with David Parry, in the productions of the *PLS* since 1976.

MEMBERS OF THE CONFERENCE

Ashley Crandell Amos, *University of Toronto*
Gabrielle Bailey, *University of Waterloo*
G.E. Bentley, Jr., *University of Toronto*
David Bevington **Speaker** *University of Chicago*
Kenneth Blackwell, *McMaster University*
William Blissett, *University of Toronto*
Laurel Braswell, *McMaster University*
Marianne G. Briscoe, *Chicago*
Sharon Butler, *University of Toronto*
Shirley Carnahan, *University of Colorado, Boulder*
John Cartwright, *University of Capetown*
John C. Coldewey, *University of Washington*
James W. Cook, *Albion College*
Audrey Douglas, *Records of Early English Drama*
Alvin I. Dust, *University of Waterloo*
JoAnna Dutka, *University of Toronto*
Robert Edwards, SUNY – *Buffalo*
John Elliott, *Syracuse University*
Goldwin S. French, *Victoria University*
David Galloway, *University of New Brunswick*
Alice Hamilton, *University of Winnipeg*
Wyman H. Herendeen, *University of Toronto*
F. David Hoeniger, *University of Toronto*
Reginald W. Ingram, *University of British Columbia*
Heather Jackson, *University of Toronto*
Henry D. Janzen, *University of Windsor*
A.F. Johnston **Convenor/Speaker** *University of Toronto*
Stanley J. Kahrl, *The Ohio State University*
David N. Klausner, *University of Toronto*
Anne Lancashire, *University of Toronto*
Ian Lancashire, *University of Toronto*
Richard Landon, *University of Toronto*

MEMBERS

John Leyerle, *University of Toronto*
Edward C. McGee, *University of St. Jerome's College*
Sally-Beth MacLean, *Records of Early English Drama*
Randy McLeod, *University of Toronto*
J.M.R. Margeson, *University of Toronto*
M.H. Means, *University of Dayton*
Peter Meredith **Speaker** *University of Leeds*
D.E. Moggridge, *University of Toronto*
Paul Mulholland, *University of Guelph*
Desmond Neill, *University of Toronto*
Barbara D. Palmer, *Chatham College*
David Parry **Speaker** *Cambridge University*
Roslyn G. Richek, *Norman, Oklahoma*
Milla B. Riggio, *Trinity College, Connecticut*
G.B. Shand, *York University*
J.A.B. Somerset **Speaker** *University of Western Ontario*
Eric Stanley, *Pembroke College, Oxford*
William P. Stoneman, *University of Toronto*
Prudence Tracy, *University of Toronto Press*
John Wasson, *Washington State University*
Paul White, *Bristol University*
Richard B. Zacha, *University of Texas at Arlington*

Introduction

The nineteenth Conference on Editorial Problems provided a forum for the discussion of a tightly focussed set of editorial concerns. The topic, "Editing Early English Drama: Special Problems and New Directions," grew naturally from the paper delivered by Professor Ian Lancashire at the twelfth Conference in 1976. The topic of that conference was "Editing Medieval Texts" and Professor Lancashire provided an admirable overview of the state of early drama editing in 1976.

Since 1976, the revolution in early drama studies has continued unchecked. The research being conducted by Records of Early English Drama (research reflected in two conference papers) has fundamentally changed many presuppositions about early drama. During the last eight years, as the REED volumes have begun to appear, other important publications have made their mark. The REED *Newsletter*, the more performance oriented *Middle English Theatre* journal from England, the monographs and newsletters of the *Early Drama Art and Music* series from Kalamazoo, the continuing appearance of the play manuscripts in facsimile from Leeds, the new edition of the *York Cycle* by Richard Beadle and a flood of articles, chapters of books, and conference proceedings have all contributed to our understanding of early drama. So, too, have the productions of many of the plays, in Canada, by the *Poculi Ludique Societas* and, in England, by the group of colleagues based in Leeds and Lancaster. But this scholarship has yet to be reflected in new editions of the plays. Given the unfortunate time-lag between the commissioning of an edition and its publication, none of the new editions that have appeared over the last decade really reflects the general revolution in our perceptions of the drama. R.M. Lumiansky and David Mills, the editors of the 1974 edition of the *Chester Cycle*, have gone a long way to salvage the situation by publishing, in 1983, a series of essays that incorporate much of the new scholarship, including their own. Richard Beadle struggled valiantly with his *York* edition, working closely with those of us editing the *York Records* on the other side of the Atlantic.

The papers contained in this volume are an attempt to stand back and assess some of the recent developments in the field and reflect on how they affect the editing of the surviving texts. The first paper by David Bevington provides an overview of earlier editions, particularly of the anthologies that have so shaped our understanding of the corpus of early drama. He demonstrates clearly how the choice of episodes to be anthologized was skewed by the historical presuppositions and religious persuasion of the generation that made the choice. He also reminds us forcibly that, in a field as specialized as this, with a corpus as large as it is, we must grapple with the economic realities of the cost of publication and the size of the audience. My own paper, the last in this collection, returns to this problem and suggests a possible solution.

The two papers that follow, by David Parry and Peter Meredith, address some of the vexatious details of editing early drama. David Parry tackles the problematic presence of Latin marginalia in the manuscript of *The Castle of Perseverance* and argues that one way to determine whether a Latin phrase is a gloss or integral to the text is to perform the play. Although his paper is limited to *The Castle*, his analysis can be applied to many manuscripts that have come down to us because he asks important questions about the nature of many early drama manuscripts and attempts some answers. Peter Meredith's paper struggles with stage directions. Using both modern and continental medieval examples before turning to English texts, he poses fundamental questions about the nature of the stage directions that are contained in early drama manuscripts. He urges that editors should treat the non-textual evidence such as the marginal and interlineated comments with the same rigour and seriousness as the texts themselves.

The last two papers, those of J.A.B. Somerset and my own, are concerned with the relationship between records evidence and the editing of dramatic texts. Alan Somerset argues that the more evidence we have of the possibilities for playing places and details of productions (even if divorced from any known text) the more editors of the surviving texts will be able to place their work in a secure context of performance practice. My own paper begins with a discussion of the relationship between the records of Chester and York and the texts of the cycles. It then moves into a more general discussion of the problems of editing such a complex corpus as that of early drama in a way that is easily accessible to colleagues and students, thus returning the conference to where it had begun with David Bevington's paper.

I hope that the papers will convey the extraordinary sense of excitement and collegiality that informed the conference. The participants included a good mixture of established scholars in the field and interested graduate students. It was a meeting of friends as well as a meeting of minds. I am grateful to all those who participated for it was the participants who, in the end, made the conference into a special event.

Particular thanks must go to the Social Sciences and Humanities Research Council of Canada, to the President's Office of the University of Toronto, to the Department of English and to University College for the financial support that made it possible to hold the conference and to publish its proceedings. I am also grateful to Victoria College for providing the site for the conference and to the *Poculi Ludique Societas* for both delighting us and instructing us with *Wit and Science* as a banquet interlude. A convenor as distracted by other concerns as myself must have strong support from others if the whole venture is not to collapse. I wish to thank the various members of the Conference Committee for their help and advice. Heather Jackson's organizational talents had mapped a clear road to follow while Sharon Butler's experience as registrar and keeper of accounts served us well. Desmond Neill as acting chairman of the Conference Committee for 1982-83 and G.E. Bentley, Jr., the chairman for 1981-82 and 1983-84, proved firm counsellors as did Prudence Tracy. But my most heartfelt thanks must go to William Stoneman, my colleague at Victoria, who, as the one responsible for local arrangements, bore the largest share of the immediate responsibility for the Conference. Finally, I must thank Lorna Cross, my secretary at Victoria, and the staff of Records of Early English Drama who, as always, cheerfully undertook the extra tasks their boss asked them to do. No boss has been better served.

The typesetting of this volume has been done by William Rowcliffe of the REED staff. I am most grateful for his willingness, and that of my Associate Editor Sally-Beth MacLean, to fit this extra task in around their regular work.

AFJ
1984

Drama Editing and Its Relation to Recent Trends in Literary Criticism

David Bevington

O.B. Hardison has shown us how Karl Young's *Drama of the Medieval Church*, for all its remarkable achievement in gathering together so many liturgical texts and Latin church dramas, reflected significant critical distortions of its era.[1] Despite his own uneasiness in doing so, Young chose to organize his two-volume edition by genre and liturgical occasion rather than according to chronology, proceeding from the liturgy of the mass and the canonical office to dramatic aspects of the liturgy and thence to Easter tropes, the visit to the sepulchre in various "stages" from simple to complex, the *Ludus Paschalis*, other plays of the Easter season, and the full Passion play, before turning in his second volume to Nativity drama and then plays dealing with other biblical and legendary subjects.

The effect, as Hardison has so acutely observed, was to underscore the Darwinian assumptions of late nineteenth-century literary criticism, in which Western drama was assumed to have grown in orderly stages, slowly assimilating material by a process of experimentation and "mutation," adding vernacular as it became more popular, daring to be comic as it ventured forth from the church into the churchyard and the town, choosing to be secular as its auspices became secular rather than religious. Hardison has shown the chronological rearrangement necessary to argue such a hypothesis, and the serious critical consequences of assuming such an antipathy between the secular and the religious. He might have added that Young's work, in its general neglect of staging matters, also reflects the penchant of philological scholarship in the nineteenth and early twentieth centuries to regard medieval dramatic texts as literary curiosities collected by antiquaries rather than as documents in the history of theatrical production.

I focus on Hardison's analysis of Young because it shows how influential an editor of medieval dramatic texts can be in reflecting and in shaping anew the cultural vision of an age. This influence is especially powerful when, as in the case of Young, the editor brings together many dramatic texts and must then arrange and select. Young made his mark not only on his own students at Yale but on those who, like Hardin Craig, wrote the history of medieval drama according to the evolutionary concepts encapsulated in Young's editing.[2] Modern editions of single texts, such as Early English Text Society editions of the various individual English cycles, are capable of their own distortions, of course, and we will be considering the consequences of a philological emphasis at the expense of theatrical interpretation. For the present, however, I should like to continue with something that, perhaps, represents a larger danger. The collection or anthology becomes the guide to literary history for its many users. Professors may shape their course around the anthology's scheme of organization, and impressionable students may discover a supposed pattern of development in such a book more readily than in historical essays or books. The plays are there, arranged and categorized in a way that compels attention. The anthology, like the curriculum, determines canon and at least implies, if it does not openly state, a sequence of literary indebtedness.

For English drama of the later Middle Ages, no anthology can excel the historical importance of A.W. Pollard's *English Miracle Plays, Moralities and Interludes* (Oxford, originally published 1890, eighth edition in 1927) and John M. Manly's two-volume *Specimens of the Pre-Shaksperean Drama* published by Ginn in 1897. Prior to and during that time, anthologies of Coussemaker (1860), Du Méril (1849, 1897), and others had encompassed smaller dramatic limits, such as liturgical drama in France or Latin origins of modern theatre.[3] Dodson's *Select Collection of Old Plays* (1744, 1780) had not ventured much before 1500. Francis J. Child's edition of *Four Old Plays* (1848) began with *Thersytes* and *Jack Juggler*. John Payne Collier's *Five Miracle Plays, or Scriptural Dramas* (1836) sampled briefly from the cycles and the Brome MS, but offered no basis for historical development. William Marriott's *Collection of English Miracle-Plays or Mysteries* (Basle, 1838) offered ten selections from the Chester, Coventry and Towneley cycles, with two of later date, again scarcely comprehensive or historical in scope. The individual cycles and other plays in manuscripts, including the Digby and Macro collections, appeared under the aegis of the Early English Text Society as artifacts of the Catholic pre-Reformation, safeguarded from public curiosity by the prophylactic apparatus of the old-spelling, critical edition.

What Pollard and Manly offered were anthologies for serious literary study, edited at Oxford and Chicago, two centres of a burgeoning movement toward philological and historical scholarship. As with Young, we must not overlook their accomplishment in our need to understand the cultural limitations of the enterprise. Pollard's collection came to include (some of these works relegated to appendices) the Harley

Harrowing of Hell (fourteenth century), a St Nicholas Play, the *Mysterium Resurrectionis Domini Nostri Jesu Christi* (Orléans, thirteenth century), extracts from the Brome *Abraham and Isaac*, five pageants from the major cycles (abridged in some cases), and considerably abridged versions of the Digby *Mary Magdalene* and of *The Castle of Perseverance* before turning to *Everyman* and Humanist drama. Pollard's 1890 preface alluded to "the small attention at that time paid to the subject in histories of English literature," and hoped that his collection might be inexpensively available and useful "to many lovers of literature unable to make the subject their special study." The book suffered poor sales at first, Pollard writes, until "large orders for it came regularly from the United States," and to a lesser degree from Germany, eventually creating the demand for subsequent editions.

The first of Manly's two volumes provided by far the most comprehensive coverage to date. It begins with brief liturgical texts from the *Regularis Concordia* and the Winchester Troper, an Easter *Visitatio* from the fourteenth century (Dublin), and the vernacular Shrewsbury fragments (fifteenth century). Its section on the cycles includes some fourteen pageants from Norwich, the Brome MS and Coventry as well as the four major cycles. The Digby *Mary Magdalene* is not there, but we have instead the Digby *Conversion of St Paul*, and the *Play of the Sacrament*. Instead of *Perseverance* we find *Mankind*, and there are Robin Hood and other folk plays before the collection turns to Humanist drama. Simply in terms of the amount provided, we are given an impressive 352 pages of text before the sixteenth century (if one allows folk drama, of later provenance, to be included in this total). Extensive study of early drama was beginning to be possible in our professional graduate schools.

On the other side, however, we can see the extent to which even these serious collections condescended to their subject as a rudimentary stage in the development of later drama.

Manly's infamous title, *Specimens of the Pre-Shaksperean Drama*, implies a twofold insult: that the plays are only archeological data with which to construct the stages of evolution of a dinosaur, and that their only lasting value in such an archeological reconstruction is to discover in it the subsequent flourishing of more advanced forms. Pollard similarly uses the phrase "specimens of the pre-Elizabethan drama" in his subtitle and in the Preface to his 1927 edition. Manly was occasionally offhand with his textual work in a way that he would not have been, I think, with the esteemed Chaucer; for instance, Manly entrusted to an *emanuensis* the transcription of *Mankind* rather than go overseas himself for the purpose, and the resulting textual collation is, in numerous instances, unintentionally hilarious.[4] Manly omits the "vulgar" Christmas ditty-songs by the revelers without clearly indicating that he is doing so while other obscenities are allowed to stand. Their impact on unwary readers is considerably softened, however, by absence of glossing.

Selection of individual texts in Pollard and Manly is heavily weighted toward the pre-Shakespearean. Pollard gives us no liturgical drama, and his earliest text is the "*Ludus super Iconia Sancti Nicolai*" from about 1125. Manly moves at once from two liturgical texts to a fourteenth-century sample of the *Visitatio*, as though the late date were of no consequence, and the Shrewsbury Fragments that so strongly urge the importance of vernacular translation. In their selections from the cycles, Pollard and Manly both avoid the entire Crucifixion sequence and, of course, the Ascensions of Christ and the Virgin in favour of subjects typologically suitable to Protestant readers: the Creation, Noah's Flood, Abraham and Isaac, Balaak and Balaam, the Salutation and Birth, the Slaughter of the Innocents, and then, leaping ahead, the Resurrection, Antichrist, and the Judgment. The *Conversion of St Paul* and the story of Mary Magdalene are the most palatable saints' stories, as they were to the Reformation, and the morality play commands attention for its role in the development of popular drama through which the troupes prepared the way for the high Renaissance.

Joseph Quincy Adams' *Chief Pre-Shakespearean Drama*, first published in 1924 by Houghton Mifflin, undertakes "to tell, as clearly as may be in selections, the story of the origin and development of the English drama." Adams apologizes for his having had "to include a few liturgical plays from the Continent, since the corresponding English plays, though known to have existed, have not survived" (Preface). This is the textbook through which many of us first encountered early drama in a serious way, for it remained in use well into the 1960's and 70's, owing in part to the untimely death of Helge Kokeritz at Yale who was to have revised it for Houghton Mifflin in the 1950's. Despite his apology for the liturgical material, Adams does provide considerably more than was in Manly. Still, its scheme of organization relies heavily on Manly (who was Adams' teacher) and on Young. Its "sources of liturgical drama" offers tropes from St Gall (tenth century), Durham, and Tours, France, obscuring the wide fluctuations of dating here in footnotes devoid of chronological information. The more "primitive form" of the *Regularis Concordia* is cited but not illustrated. A section on Easter liturgical drama, much like Manly's, jumps unchronologically from the tenth-century *Regularis* text to fifteenth-century Dublin to thirteenth-century Orléans to fourteenth-century Rouen. What is created out of this eclectic procedure is the appearance of an Easter play that develops by accretion, adding the lament of the three Marys, then the race to the tomb, then a more elaborate sepulchre, intricate choral singing, and so on, as it continues to "grow," followed in due course by new Easter subjects and other characters such as the *Peregrini*, the midwives, the Magi, and, triumphantly, the comic King Herod (though the Herod so latterly introduced might, in fact, have been found in the twelfth-century Fleury MS). Other Latin church drama in Adams gives prominence to the *Ordo Prophetarum*, then thought to be seminal in the genesis of the cycles, three St Nicholas plays with their attractively nonbiblical and sensational subject matter, and the *Conversion of St Paul*. A whole section, though brief, is devoted to the "introduction of the vernacular," insisting on the primacy and logically precise significance of this forward-looking event.

Adams' presentation of the craft cycles, though more extensive than that of any preceding anthology, reinforces a disproportionate emphasis on Old Testament typological subjects from Genesis and the *Ordo Prophetarum*, together with a dislike for the Ascension plays. Adams does commendably present the beginning of the Crucifixion sequence from N-Town, but breaks off well before the Crucifixion itself and does not venture the York dramatization of this subject. Indeed, the next event is the Harrowing of Hell and the Resurrection, followed by a long jump to the York Judgment. Offensive phrases are omitted *causa pudoris*. The more this edition moves toward real accessibility to students, in fact, with its translations of the Latin and its glossaries, the more fearful it becomes of scenes and language offensive to Protestant sensibilities. It is not at all squeamish about printing the attacks on Jesus' tormentors as a "vile race of Jews, Whom a dire madness makes frenzied" (Orléans *Sepulchrum*, p 15), a text that has more recently created a great deal of adverse publicity for productions of medieval church drama,[5] but Adams' edition turns blushingly away from the Crucifixion and Deposition with their vivid icons of the bleeding God.

The abridgement of *Mary Magdalene* clearly approaches the text in a similar fashion, retaining the story of Christ's ministry and Mary's penitent conversion (so nicely parallel to that of St Paul) while excising the long so-called second half (in fact, a seamless continuation) with its lurid miracles and romantic travels and bogus imitation of the life and Ascension of Christ. The inclusion of folk drama and *Dux Moraud* give prominence to the secular. The version of *The Castle of Perseverance* is extensively cut, presumably to make it less tedious. *Mankind* is there, but bowdlerized more than in Manly. If Adams' edition is not exactly the "family" pre-Shakespearean drama, on the model of the "family" Shakespeare, it does what it can to move in that direction. Most importantly, perhaps, the overall design of the book argues that pre-1500 drama is something less than half the story of pre-Shakespearean drama, and that all English and much continental drama back to the tenth century finds its justification in the study of literature as an anticipation of Falstaff and Iago and Doctor Faustus. Such was the lesson one could scarcely have avoided, in higher education, as late as 1975.

When I was first approached, around 1961, with the idea of revising Adams' anthology, I expect that Houghton Mifflin, and I too, at the start, supposed that the revision would be not extensive. No one in my acquaintance knew what we had been missing. Graduate education at Harvard paid virtually no attention to the whole of the Latin Middle Ages, dramatic or nondramatic, and graduate students were encouraged to think of bibliographical training as a kind of curious luxury or sideline. One index of the Protestant Whig-Liberal bias in graduate education of the day, at Harvard and elsewhere, is that Roman Catholics were appointed to faculty positions about as frequently as women and blacks. Moreover, I wanted to keep those fine plays at the end of Adams' anthology, which are, I regret, now less available than they were: Richard Edwards' *Damon and Pythias*, Lyly's *Campaspe*, the anonymous *Famous Victories of Henry the Fifth*, and *George a Greene, the Pinner of Wakefield*. I felt less regret about giving up *Roister Doister, Gammer Gurton's Needle, Gorboduc*, and *Supposes*, because they were and are available in Elizabethan drama anthologies by Baskerville *et al*, Fraser and Rabkin, and still others.[6] When at a late date Heywood's *Four PP* fell under the axe, on the other hand, I grieved. Moreover, I had at one time included, and, in fact, fully prepared for the printer, texts of Medwall's *Fulgens and Lucrece* and Skelton's *Magnyfycence* that subsequently had to be removed. These excisions came after the manuscript had been fully submitted and accepted at Houghton Mifflin; I was told by an embarrassed Vice-President that they (I too) had underestimated length and costs, and that the manuscript would have to be cut by 250-300 pages. How can one justify taking out *Four PP* and *Fulgens and Lucrece* to make room for an uncut *Castle of Perseverance* and the second "half" of *Mary Magdalene*? Clearly Mr Adams and I had parted company by this time on what an anthology of early drama was for.

The overwhelming question for this edition, then, had to be one of selection, because selection implied so much about how medieval drama should be taught and studied. I wished, and wish still, that editing need not take such a managerial and codifying role. Ideally, all early drama texts would be cheaply available in any combination as one might wish, so that ideas of canonicity might continue to change. I was anxious to include an entire English cycle so that it might be studied as an artistic whole. I wanted to include several examples of a single episode from the cycles, such as Noah, to permit comparative study. I especially wanted to include more continental church drama, and at one point had a fully prepared text and translation both of the Montecassino Passion Play and the Tegernsee *Antichrist*. I looked longingly at continental saints' plays on so many subjects, at the Cornish *Ordinalia*, at the French morality play – why not include a really comprehensive text of some 36,000 lines? – and at the individual pageants from England not in the major four cycles. I worked hard on folk drama and secular fragments like *Dux Moraud* and the *Interludium de Clerico et Puella*, and planned to include them as Manly and Adams had done. Why not, as long as I was dreaming, include some of the lost dramatic literature of the Middle ages? Still to come on such a list was Dutch bourgeois drama existing in such profusion.

In reality, editing a single volume covering such a large corpus necessitated severe limitations that had not been faced previously, since no anthology had been devoted to medieval drama as such. Once the goal of identifying medieval drama in its own right rather than as pre-Shakespearean drama had become clear, then the fate of *Damon and Pythias* and *Campaspe*, however regrettable, became the responsibility of some other editing project. As I read Young's *Drama of the Medieval Church*, side by side with Hardison and Arnold Williams, (Rosemary Woolf, V.A. Kolve and others were yet to appear when I started)[7] I saw that the space freed by the abandonment of late sixteenth-century drama needed to be devoted heavily to early liturgical ceremonials and plays, arranged as nearly as possible in chronological rather than topical order, and to church drama of the twelfth-century renaissance. I inevitably felt the pull toward "development" in the drama, since space would not allow undue repetition of essentially similar tropes or ceremonials and hence the very demonstration of varying forms tended to emphasize what had been "added" to the *Visitatio* original. Still, in a section on tenth-century versions of the Visit to the Sepulchre, I felt it necessary to show that four texts, arranged in probably chronological order, gave second place to the simplest extant trope from St Gall and third place to the considerably more elaborate extraliturgical ceremony from the *Regularis Concordia*. Similarly in Christmas drama the Fleury Herod Play, with its extraordinary portrait of Herod, suggests how early we find fully developed Christmas plays instead of a number of orderly stages from the Visit of the Shepherds to the Visit of the Magi. (Adams' *Pastores* play, textually originating from Rouen in the fourteenth century but "which came into existence not later than the eleventh century," is an example of his chronological straitjacketing to give the appearance of evolution.) The section on music drama in the twelfth century is designed to represent the extraordinary variety and achievement of drama at that comparatively early date, with and without the assistance of the vernacular and of outdoor staging techniques; the Anglo-Norman *Adam* is there, and *La Seinte Resureccion*, along with the Latin *Play of Daniel*, Hilarius' *Raising of Lazarus*, the Benedicktbeuern Christmas play, and others, demonstrating splendour of production, versification, and characterization both inside and outside the church building.

Anthologizing the Corpus Christi cycles cannot avoid some compromise. I accepted the inevitability of a composite cycle, trusting that teachers could direct students to available editions of a complete cycle for more extensive work in a single text. I certainly do that when I teach medieval drama. In the composite version in the anthology I have put considerable emphasis on the Passion sequence, so truncated in earlier anthologies, and have tried to give long sequences from various cycles such as the N-Town Passion Play sequence and the Wakefield version of the Nativity story beginning with the Annunciation (although with an excursion into York for the Birth and Shepherds in order to facilitate a comparison between these related cycles). I concluded that a composite, anthologized cycle needs to focus on what Kolve calls the protocycle of plays appearing in all or most of the individual cycles, in order that students might perceive typological recurrences and principles of selection in the formation of the cycles, and so the emphasis falls on the Creation, Adam and Eve, Cain and Abel, Noah, Abraham and Isaac, Moses, the Prophets, the Nativity sequences, the Raising of Lazarus, the Passion story, the Harrowing of Hell, the Resurrection, the Appearances to the Disciples, and the Last Judgment.

The obvious cost of such a prototype is not only its composite nature but its ignoring of more idiosyncratic material. Although this collection makes a gesture toward atypical drama in the N-Town Woman Taken in Adultery, it does not include any of the apocryphal life of Mary so prominent in N-Town, or the fine Antichrist plays from Chester (Chester in general is underrepresented), or plays found outside the four major cycles other than the Brome Abraham and Isaac, or, still more idiosyncratically, the story of Seth's quest for the oil of mercy and the legend of the cross from the Cornish *Ordinalia*. I am distressed that the paucity of material after Christ's Resurrection gives too little attention to ascension and apocalyptic material so pointedly omitted by editors in the Protestant Whig-Liberal tradition. Conversely, an accentuation of the Wakefield Master's art (only the First Shepherds' Pageant is omitted) deprives the collection of more normative versions; as Rosemary Woolf urges, the Wakefield Master's Judgment play vividly satirizes damnation at the expense of the more usual emphasis on God's great mercy toward mankind,[8] and the Chester Noah gives us an emphasis on staging devices that nicely offsets the humorous characterization of the Wakefield version. Is the inclusion of so much of the Wakefield Master a vestige of the pre-Shakespearean conception? One could well argue that it is.

The major bias of the latter part of the volume, at any rate, is that it ignores continental drama almost entirely. *Mary Magdalene* and *The Conversion of St Paul* are hardly typical saints' plays, and may indeed owe their very survival to their acceptability in Protestant eyes; to shape a view of conversion-drama on them alone is probably not even to represent what English drama was attempting in the fifteenth century. Certainly the evidence accumulating in the REED project casts doubts on the centrality of the morality plays to which the final section of this anthology gives so many pages. Continental drama is present only as adapted to the English scene, as in *Everyman* and John Heywood's *John John*, and hence the anthology is once more vulnerable on the old grounds of seeking a pathway to the stage of Shakespeare and his contemporaries. I can only conclude this intriguing assignment of writing my own book review by assuring you that I pondered the alternatives and that I really do hope that the editing of medieval texts in anthologies will soon have an opportunity to define the obsolescence of my undertaking in much the way that I have defined that of my predecessors. Literary criticism and editing do not "evolve" in a Darwinian sense any more than medieval drama; let us hope that we are beyond assuming that change is to be equated with progress. Change is, on the other hand, an inevitable condition of literary criticism and editing. To apply great things to small, Spenser's *Cantos of Mutability* do suggest a pattern in the history of criticism and editing whereby a glimpse of what is "eterne" can be obtained only through incessant quest and replacement. The cost of producing books may hinder the process – Houghton Mifflin, I can tell you, reviewed and very nearly abandoned this anthology project long after it had first agreed to publish, and finally went ahead only with a cut-back manuscript and an arrangement to print the text in South Korea. Still, the rising costs of all texts of medieval drama, including the cycles, renders it imperative that some selected presentation of texts be available for the classroom and seminar. The editing of anthologies cannot avoid its function as a product of current criticism and as a significant shaper of the way in which these texts will be studied in the future.

I should like to say just a word about stage directions. They are to be the subject of other discussions in this volume, and we are all eager to respond to the challenge formulated by this forum of redressing the philological balance so woefully needed in the format of the EETS editions. Stanley Kahrl's reviews have for years taken the EETS to task on this score, as have my own reviews and those of other scholars.[9] I sense such a unanimity of knife-sharpening, in fact, that my inclination is to utter a word of warning on the other side. My editing, both of medieval drama and of Shakespeare, has pushed me in two irreconcilable directions: toward providing fuller information on stage movement, gesture, structures, and the like, in bracketed editorial stage direction, and toward an awareness that one can very easily assert what is questionable, unknowable, or hard to place with precision.

In my eagerness to tell more about kneeling, clasping of hands, crossing the acting area, and the like, I was unprepared for the response of the theatrical people to whom I showed my first efforts. I thought they at least would welcome attention to staging matters. Not a bit of it. And, in the main, they are right to urge caution. The business of providing gesture and motion belongs to the actors, they insist. They are not merely being proprietary, telling scholars to stay out, as theatrical people sometimes do. The real danger they observe is in closing off alternatives. Once one asserts, in an official-looking stage direction, however bracketed, that a character kneels at one point and rises at another, one is asserting that the actor could not have risen five lines later, or refused to kneel despite the implications of the language, or treated the whole thing as a joke.

The use of historical sources to supply questionable stage directions can be illustrated from J. Dover Wilson's edition of *1 Henry* IV, Act V, scene iv. Wilson's opening stage direction specifies that Prince Hal enters "*wounded in the cheek.*" The source for this added stage business is Holinshed, who reports that Hal "was hurt in the face with an arrow." Shakespeare does not mention this fact, though clearly he knew Holinshed well. Did he intend that the actor of Hal follow history? The specificity here is not unlike that practiced by editors in search of location of Shakespeare's scenes. Many editors specify for example that Act III, scene i of the same play occurs at the house of the Archdeacon of Bangor because Holinshed places a meeting there of the deputies of Hotspur, Glendower, and Lord Mortimer. Shakespeare's unhistorical meeting of the three lords themselves makes no mention of the Archdeacon's house, and seems, instead, to imply that we are at Glendower's house, for Glendower is very much the host of the occasion.

Recent editorial opinion condemns the use of history to "correct" Shakespeare's scene. Should we not also be wary of adding stage business based on historical accounts not mentioned by the dramatist? Certainly no one would object to a director using the information, or to an editor's including it in his commentary, but does not an added stage direction bespeak a canonicity of textual accuracy that is misleading here? Many editors' false "conservatism" in retaining traditional stage business added by editors and not in the original text should warn us that stage directions, even when bracketed, may indeed become canonical.

Added stage directions tend to be reductive rather that liberating. Obviously there is an important place for some of them, and we do need, in fact, to try to hazard guesses as carefully as we can and then ask subsequent editors to be unsparingly critical. Certainly we ourselves need to be wholly sceptical of all editorially added stage directions that have come before. The "conservative" tendency of regarding them as part of the original text is deeply ingrained and is wholly without justification. Let us remember, however, as we press forward in an attempt to make our texts more consciously theatrical, that our own proneness to error will one day be self-evident.

Let us remember too, finally, that the current dicta of regarding the play-text as a script, and the play as finally realizable only in performance, are potentially as stultifying as the clichés to which philological scholarship attached itself. The manuscripts we edit were not uniformly regarded as play scripts by those who wrote and copied them. Some of them, at least, were works of art to be preserved in collections and savoured as treasures for the eye. The editor of such manuscripts loses something essential when he regards them as nothing more than blueprints for performance, and a modern editor cannot afford to lose sight of his responsiblity imposed upon him by this great consideration.

NOTES

1. O.B. Hardison, Jr., *Christian Rite and Christian Drama in the Middle Ages*, Baltimore, 1965, Essay 1; Karl Young, *The Drama of the Medieval Church*, 2 vols., Oxford, 1933.
2. Hardin Craig, *English Religious Drama of the Middle Ages*, Oxford, 1955.
3. Edmond de Coussemaker, *Drames liturgiques du Moyen Age*, Rennes, 1860, facsimile, New York, 1964, and Edelestand Du Méril, *Origines latines du Théâtre moderne*, Paris, 1849, reprinted in facsimile, Paris, 1897.
4. See the collations in David Bevington, ed., *The Macro Plays*, New York, Johnson Reprint, Washington, 1972, pp 254–305.
5. The production of the Benediktbeuern Passion Play, mounted in March 1982 at Indiana University by Clifford Flanigan, Thomas Binkley and others, and taken to the Cloisters in New York, aroused such an outcry from the Jewish community that the Director of the Metropolitan Museum issued a public apology.
6. Charles Read Baskervill, Virgil B. Heltzel and Arthur H. Nethercot, eds., *Elizabethan Plays*, New York, 1934, rev. ed. 1971, and Russell A. Fraser and Norman Rabkin, eds., *Drama of the English Renaissance I: The Tudor Period*, New York, 1976.
7. Arnold Williams, *The Drama of Medieval England*, East Lansing, 1961, Rosemary Woolf, *The English Mystery Plays*, Berkeley, 1972, and V.A. Kolve, *The Play Called Corpus Christi*, London, 1966.
8. Woolf, *The English Morality Plays*, p 295.
9. See my review of *Non-Cycle Plays and Fragments*, ed. Norman Davis, in *Speculum*, XLVI (1971), pp 733–36.

A Margin of Error:
The Problems of Marginalia in
The Castle of Perseverance

David Parry

Whilst checking through the penultimate draft of this paper and making some minor revisions, I came across a cryptic note in one of the margins of my typescript. It read simply, "depend on Latin." I looked at the note for a moment, and then remembered why I had put it there. The argument at that point in the paper depends on the assumption that at least part of a medieval audience for *The Castle of Perseverance* would have understood what was actually being said in one of the Latin tag lines which crop up with some frequency in the manuscript play-text. Reading over the paper two or three days earlier I had felt this dependence needed rather more emphasis, and had pencilled the words in the margin to remind myself to insert a sentence or two in the relevant paragraph when next at the typewriter.

"Depend on Latin" – the words make perfect sense when the opportunity exists to explain them in this way. But one wonders what a reader of the typescript five hundred years or so hence would make of them, if that penultimate draft of the paper with all its pencilled notes, emendations, and *aides memoires* happened to be the only version to survive the ravages of time. The note appears in the margin alongside a passage which discusses various interpretations of a particular Latin tag – "*Sapientia penes domini*"[1] – and concludes with a sentence which reads, "other, even more convoluted explanations are, I am sure, possible."[2] Now what on earth would a future reader make of the marginal note at that point without the present explanation to guide him? "Depend on Latin" – a somewhat sarcastic reference to the propensity of the Latin language for confusing the issue? Or a cheerful note of reassurance that, despite the convolutions, Latin would naturally make everything clear in the end? I don't know. But I do suspect that, whatever the interpretations put upon the note, this little item amongst my own textual marginalia would probably cause the same kinds of problems to those hypothetical future readers as the various marginalia in *The Castle of Perseverance* manuscript have caused me over the past three or four years, during which time I have first directed a production, and more recently prepared a new critical edition of this fascinating early English play.[3]

In August, 1979, *The Castle of Perseverance* was staged in its entirety at the University of Toronto. This production was the first, and as far as I know, remains to date the only complete presentation of the play in modern times.[4] For the Toronto production a modernized acting text was prepared by Professor Alexandra F. Johnston and myself, using Mark Eccles's 1969 edition of the play as a textual base.[5] Our modernization was conservative, and attempted not only to create an acceptable modern acting version of the original text in its entirety, but also to reproduce as far as possible the original metrical and alliterative patterns, rhyme schemes, and other features of the then-accepted text such as the extra-metrical Latin tags scattered throughout the play. These latter, like the macaronic phrases of Latin and Old French encountered within the verse text, we left untranslated, intending them to be spoken in the original language by the actors in performance. The approach to the spoken text described here reflects the orientation and the intentions of the production as a whole. Just as in its staging the production was intended to test to the fullest extent possible the validity of then-current theories regarding the original method of mounting the play, so too in its textual way it was intended to test to the limit the theatrical and dramatic qualities of the play text when performed uncut and unmodified in structure. The production, in other words, was planned as a thorough and comprehensive piece of practical research into the nature of the play in all its aspects.

The process of rehearsal proved the new acting text to be, on the whole, a sound and workmanlike version of the play. The Toronto cast responded to it with enthusiasm, and were generally able to speak it with ease and fluency. Naturally, not everything in the text worked perfectly from the outset; difficulties were encountered with many individual passages and words in the new version. But since both Professor Johnston and myself were on hand throughout the production, we were able to make revisions on the spot, giving a more workable shape to lines and phrases which proved awkward in delivery and finding new synonyms for occasional words which for various reasons failed to convey fully their intended meaning.

With some of the Latin lines, however, we had a good deal more difficulty. During the process of rehearsal it became increasingly clear that in the majority of cases those Latin lines which lay outside the verse structure were impeding the flow of the play in a variety of ways. No amount of careful rehearsal seemed to obviate this. The problem did not appear to be related to any difficulty which might have been anticipated with the actors speaking the Latin. Many of them came to the production with at least some grounding in the language.

Even those who did not found no real difficulty, after some guidance with pronunciation, in dealing effectively with the Latin incorporated into the normal metrical and rhyme schemes of the verse text and using it for its intended dramatic effect. Rather, the problem seemed to lie in the nature of the play-text itself.

In almost every case, when an extra-metrical Latin line was delivered by the actor the perceived effect was of a disruption of the poetic and dramatic rhythms the playwright had established. In many instances the content of the line seemed also to disrupt the flow of thought or argument the character speaking had been pursuing.[6] And in one instance the text of a Latin tag appeared flatly to contradict the physical action clearly required by every other piece of contextual evidence at that point in the script.[7] There were exceptions: all the extra-metrical lines which appeared to belong to God's speeches,[8] and one which appeared to be part of a speech by Mercy,[9] seemed to fit their context both in rhythm and meaning, and gave neither the actors nor their auditors in rehearsal any difficulty.

Faced with the dramaturgical and directorial problem I have outlined here, a choice clearly had to be made: to retain all these troublesome lines in the acting text and try to make them work somehow in performance; or to cut the lines and risk a possible major distortion of the effect the playwright had intended. I was initially very much opposed to cutting a substantial part (some thirty-nine lines) of a text which had been established on sound editorial principles simply because our own performance technique and production aesthetic could not accommodate themselves to those for which the play had presumably been written. Such a course seemed altogether too subjective and arbitrary, and in direct contradiction of our concern for scrupulous scholarly investigation of the effects of the original text in performance. However, despite further careful experimentation in rehearsal, no way could be found to make the problem lines work within the terms the play itself seemed to lay down.[10]

At this point I returned to the sources. All existing editions and commentaries were re-examined to see if there might not be a question of authenticity in regard to any of the Latin tag lines. Every edition included the lines as part of the play-text proper. Critical commentary was silent on the subject, with a single exception: Michael J. Kelley argued that the lines were part of what he termed the play's "flamboyant ornamental figuration," and integral to the text.[11] Examination of the manuscript facsimile, however, revealed some interesting details. Of the thirty-nine problem lines, twenty-eight were in a marginal position. While they were in the same scribal hand as the rest of the copy, their physical relationship to the text as a whole suggested that they might perhaps in a prior copy have been annotations, and not lines in the play at all.[12] The remaining extra-metrical lines, however, were written just as if they were part of the stanzaic verse form of the play and were intended to be spoken. Clearly, since there was no simple correlation between the lines which were causing difficulty and a marginal position, no consistent argument regarding their authenticity could be applied. The dramaturgical choice was thus in many ways now more difficult. The play was well into rehearsal, and there was insufficient time, at that point, for a detailed study of the manuscript and for fresh textual analysis which might have proved the authenticity or otherwise of the offending lines. Yet I had to do something.

Based on our rehearsal experience with the text thus far, I made an editorial guess and decided to eliminate from the acting version all those extra-metical lines which appeared in the manuscript as if they might be non-textual marginalia. All the other extra-metrical Latin tags I retained. The emendations actually made to the text up to the time of performance and the reasons for making those emendations were discussed in the programme notes for the production.[13] It is, I believe, fair to say that in simple practical terms those dubious lines which were allowed to stand as part of the acting text remained problematic in rehearsal and performance. It is also fair to say that the textual uncertainty generated by this experience with the Latin tags led to a more general attitude of scepticism on my own part regarding the soundness of the established text as a whole, and to a great curiosity as to the real nature of what had been transmitted to us in *The Castle of Perseverance* manuscript. As a result, many more elements of the text were called into question during the production process than might otherwise have been the case. Some problematic stage directions in particular came in for severe critical reassessment. Here too, however, a comprehensive reappraisal of the corpus of stage directions and staging annotations contained in the manuscript had to wait until the production itself was over and there was time to devote to a full scholarly study of the problems.

For lack of space, I do not intend to deal at any length with the stage directions in the present paper. I shall, however, refer to the questions they raise. As part of the extensive and varied marginalia of the text, the problem of their interpretation is closely linked to that of the Latin lines, and to the way in which those lines have come to form part of the manuscript.[14]

The problem of the Latin tags is a complex one. Like most manuscripts of medieval English play-texts, that of *The Castle* contains a fair amount of Latin. Much of this is found in the form of stage directions and speech headings – a phenomenon familiar from most other dramatic manuscripts of the period. Much of the rest takes the form of Latin quotations and short phrases which are clearly a part of the text the author[15] intended his actors to speak. Such quotations are carefully integrated into the stanzas of which they form a part, and conform to them in rhyme and metre. This is the case, for example, with these lines from a speech by the Bad Angel:[16]

> We schul to hell, bothe to –
> And, boy, "in inferno
> Nulla est redemptio"
> For no kynnys þynge! (3095–3098)

or with these from a speech by Truth:

> þou he cried "Mercy!" moriendo,
> Nimis tarde penitendo,
> Talem mortem reprehendo:
> Lete hym drynke as he brewyth! (3271–3274)

or these by Mercy:

> Quia dixisti "Misericordiam seruabo,"
> "Mercy" schal I synge and say,
> And "Miserere" schal I pray
> For Mankynde, euere and ay!
> Misericordias Domini in eternum cantabo!
>   (3374–3378)

The examples quoted here are particularly interesting not only for their skilful macaronic construction as such, but also for the clear demonstration they give of the playwright's ready ability to integrate Biblical and other existing texts into his normal English verse structure. He gives the Bad Angel a literal quotation from the Sarum Usage Office of the Dead: "*in inferno nulla est redemptio,*" and Mercy a similarly literal quotation from Psalm 89 in the final line quoted: "*Misericordias Domini in eternum cantabo*" – "the mercies of the Lord I will sing forever" (Psalm 89:1).[17] In the first line of Mercy's passage quoted above, however, while the playwright draws on another verse of Psalm 89 for his text, his requirements in terms of meaning and versification do not allow a simple literal quotation. He therefore takes a part of the verse (Psalm 89:28) which in the original reads "*in eternum servabo illi misericordiam meam*" – "I will keep my mercy for him forever" – and reworks it in the manner noted above: "Quia dixisti 'Misericordiam seruabo,'/ 'Mercy' schal I synge and say," – "Because you have said 'I will keep my mercy,'/ 'Mercy' shall I sing and say," and so on. The overall result is a smooth flow of rhyme, metre, and thought in these five macaronic lines which conclude the stanza. The techniques are skilful and effective.

The *Castle* playwright is, of course, not alone in using such techniques. They are common practice throughout the full range of early European drama. Many instances are found, for example, close to hand in *Mankind* and *Wisdom*, the other two plays of the Macro manuscript,[18] and numerous examples might be cited from the Cycle and Saints' plays and from the Tudor interludes. They are also found extensively used in a good deal of non-dramatic literature of the period, *Piers Plowman* being a particularly well-known and striking example in this field. A detailed analysis of the phenomenon lies entirely outside the boundaries of the present study. However, it may be fairly stated here that the author of *The Castle* exhibits at least as much sophistication in his control of the technique as we find in most other instances of its use in early English drama.

The kind of incorporation described here, in which Latin scriptural texts, glosses and other material become part of the structure of the verse in which the play is written seems not, however, to be the only way in which the playwright has integrated Latin into the spoken text. As we have noted, there is a total of forty-six lines, including one verse couplet, apparently inserted into or appended to the play-text at various points throughout its length. Like those incorporated into the verse, most are quotations from the Bible, but there are also a number from other sources. Some of these other sources, like Cato's *Distichs*,[19] have been identified, and some have not.

Every previous editor of *The Castle* has included all these extra-metrical lines in the play-text itself. The most recent editor, Peter Happé, whose edition appeared shortly after the Toronto production, does have a brief note in which he remarks of the lines that "probably they were not all meant to be delivered in performance."[20] However, Happé does not develop his argument, and he includes all the lines in his text without making any attempt to distinguish those which he considers might have been intended for delivery in performance from those which he thinks might not. Indeed, whereas Furnivall and Pollard leave the lines out of their numbering sequence entirely,[21] and both Eccles and Bevington distinguish them by giving them the number of the lines they follow with the suffix "a", Happé simply includes them in his overall line-numbering sequence without any distinguishing mark. Only Happé makes any reference to the lines being anything other than part of the play-text proper.

Of the forty-six lines under consideration, twenty-eight are written in the right-hand margin of the manuscript in positions which approximate closely to those occupied by the manuscript stage directions and staging annotations.[22] As with some of the stage directions, a number of the marginal Latin tag lines show evidence of squeezing of the scribal hand.[23] All, however, do appear to be in the handwriting of the single scribe responsible for the manuscript as a whole.[24] The other eighteen lines are written in the position of normal stanza lines on the left-hand side of the page, and without any squeezing of the hand. Of these eighteen lines, six belong to God,[25] all except one of which apparently begin a stanza. Of the other twelve lines in this group, one (Mercy's line mentioned earlier) begins a stanza,[26] eight appear to follow the last line of a stanza,[27] and three appear to follow the fourth line of a stanza.[28] Of the total of forty-six lines, seven are marked with a paragraph sign which resembles a superior *a* in the left-hand margin. Such marking, however, appears to be quite random, and examples are found in both marginal and non-marginal categories of Latin lines.[29] Finally, one occasionally finds that within a single speech, one of the Latin tags will be written in the margin and another in normal stanzaic position on the left-hand side of the page.[30]

Physically, then, there seems to be a rather random quality to the scribal treatment of these extra-metrical lines: some are written in the margin and some in the main body of the verse text; some are marked with a paragraph sign and some are not; some marginal lines are written in the scribe's normal hand while others are clearly squeezed; some single speeches of one character contain more than one of these different kinds of treatment of the Latin tags. The overall impression one derives from a survey of this evidence suggests there may well have been some doubt in the mind of the scribe as to whether or not the material in question was part of the play-text proper, and argues that we might ourselves entertain a similar doubt. Close analysis of the content of the lines provides even stronger reasons for doubting their textual authenticity.

Superficially, it might be argued, the Latin tags seem either like standard source glosses – in this case mostly of Biblical origin – or occasionally like the *themata* of a series of mini-sermons, and, as such, integral to the play text. Michael J. Kelley, as we noted earlier, has gone further and suggested not only that the lines are an integral part of the play's structure, but also that the playwright saw them as a significant part of his overall "flamboyant" design for the work.[31] Kelley has also argued that, in all but a few cases, the lines "simply restate what already is said in English, their presence not required for sense."[32] On close examination, however, the reverse proves to be true. In all but a few cases, the Latin adds a significant new dimension or direction to what has been said or is about to be said in the verse. In some cases, as we shall see, it even appears to contradict what is being said. Let me turn to some specific examples. Before doing so, however, I should stress that while I shall not attempt to examine in detail every one of the forty-six lines in question, the examples to be considered here are typical, not special cases.

The first is found quite early in the play, as part of an interchange between the Good and the Bad Angel. The former has argued that Mankind should not covet "... Werldys goode,/ Syn Criste in erthe, and hys meynye/ All in pouert here bei stode" (350–52). He concludes the stanza by telling Mankind that Christ did not seek worldly wealth, "But forsok it euery whytt./ Example I fynde in holy wryt;/ He wyl bere me wytnesse!" (359–61). The Latin tag which follows looks as if it belongs to the spoken text: it is written immediately under the final line of the stanza in the scribe's normal hand; and the rule separating the stanza to which it seems to belong from the next is drawn immediately underneath it. But the tag reads as follows: "*diuicias et paupertates ne dederis michi domine*" – "O Lord, give me neither poverty nor riches." This is not at all what might have been expected. The Good Angel has just been preaching the necessity of poverty, citing Christ as his model: clearly not the "middle way" advocated in the quotation from Proverbs 30:8. If the Latin line is indeed supposed to read as part of the play-text proper, the stanza as a whole presents an apparently insoluble problem of interpretation. The problem is not one which has arisen because of a changed sensibility: a medieval audience, however clerkly, would surely have been just as puzzled as a modern one by a Biblical quotation which seems directly in conflict with the course of action the Good Angel has just been advocating to Mankind. The tag seems completely out of place in the speech itself. It has, rather, the feel of a reflective comment on the content of the speech by someone reading the play in the study – and moreover someone who preferred the ideal of the golden mean rather than the austerity preached by the Angel.[33]

The same reflective quality may be ascribed to the quotation from Ecclesiasticus which appears to end the first speech of Folly, one of the World's servants. Folly's stanza concludes with these words:

> Werldly wyt was neuere nout,
> But wyth foly it were frawt:
> þus þe wysman hath tawt
> Abotyn in his boke. (513–16)

A Latin text then follows: "*sapientia penes domini*"[34] – "wisdom is with the lord." Like the first example we considered, this text too is written in the scribe's normal hand directly underneath the last line of the stanza proper. It thus appears physically as part of the play text. If the quotation is the playwright's work, however, it is difficult to imagine how he might have intended the scriptural reference to be understood by those in the audience who understood the Latin. Taken literally, the text flatly contradicts everything Folly has just said about the nature of "werldly wyt." If not taken literally, there are perhaps several ways in which the educated part of the audience might have interpreted the reference. They might, for instance, have assumed that the playwright was playing with the word "*domini*" and, with the addition of an appropriate gesture from the actor, having Folly blasphemously say to the audience that all wisdom resides with the World – his own *dominus*. They might, on the other hand, have assumed that the playwright was putting a deliberately contradictory misquotation into the mouth of Folly as an example to them of this character's foolishness. Or they might, just conceivably, have assumed that he was trying to create a more complex irony and, by having Folly knowingly misquote scriptural authority with the intention of misleading them, was demonstrating the character's wickedness. Other, even more convoluted explanations are, I am sure, possible. The question which must be answered, however, is not whether they are possible but whether they are at all probable in the context of performance – particularly a context of performance in which the majority of the audience probably did not understand the Latin anyway.[35] The answer must surely be "no": the tag again has the quality of a reader's comment on Folly's statement of the nature of true wisdom.

Many tag lines are found incorporated into or appended to the speeches of the Virtues during the seige of the castle. As in the two examples considered above, some of these tags seem either to contradict or else to sit very uneasily with their spoken context. After Wrath's challenge, for example, Patience replies with a stanza which begins as follows:

> Fro þi dowthe, Crist me schelde
> þis iche day, and al mankynde!
> þou wrecchyd Wrethe, wood and wylde,
> Pacyens schal þe schende!   (2121–24)

A Latin tag appears in the right-hand margin aligned with the verse text in such a way as to suggest it might be spoken after the fourth line. It reads: "*quia ira viri iusticiam dei non operatur*" – "for the anger of man worketh not the justice of God" (Jas. 1:20). This seems at first sight to fit the context both syntactically and thematically. Unfortunately, however, the verse stanza continues as follows:

> For Marys sone, meke and mylde,
> Rent þe up, rote and rynde,
> Whanne he stod, meker þanne a chylde
> And lete boyes hym betyn and bynde.   (2125–28)

In other words, we are now given the playwright's real version of Patience's argument for her confidence in ultimate victory over Wrath. This argument has no direct connection at all with the scriptural tag. The latter appears instead to be once more a commentarial addition: a perfectly valid gloss, but quite out of place as part of Patience's lines, whose flow of argument it would seriously disrupt.

Of the three tags so far considered, the first two would clearly give just as much of a problem to the reader of the play as they would to an audience witnessing a live performance. Their meaning in the context in which we find them is obscure. The meaning of the third is not obscure, and it would cause little problem, perhaps, to a reader who could take it as a parallel or parenthetical thought on the subject under discussion by Patience. To an audience at a live performance, however, I suspect the effect would be distracting and somewhat puzzling. Quite apart from the thematic disruption the tag introduces into the speech, another disruptive effect may be noted in this instance, again more noticeable to an audience than to a reader. If delivered at the point in the stanza apparently indicated by its marginal position, the tag interrupts the normal *abababab* rhyming sequence of the first part of the stanza. This creates a serious problem in terms of the dynamics of the verse, and of its delivery by the actor.

The problem referred to here is characteristic of many of the tag lines. While they may not, unlike the examples given above, be thematically disruptive, they seem seriously to disrupt the dramatic and poetic rhythms of the play. Take, for example, the quotation which follows another early speech of the Good Angel: "*homo memento finis et in eternum non peccabis*" – "*man, think on your end and you will never sin.*" This in no way contradicts or muddles the statement the Good Angel has just made, though it adds nothing to what has just been said except the weight of scriptural authority.[36] What it does, however, is to break up the poetic structure and create a measured pause at a totally inappropriate moment. The argument between the angels, and their struggle for Mankind's will, which have been building steadily and with increasing rhythmic momentum, are here fast approaching their climax.

The verse echoes the urgency of the respective approaches of the Angels to Mankind as he wavers between them:

BONUS ANGELUS

...

Man, þynke on þyn endynge day,
Whanne þou schalt be closyd vndyr clay, –
And if þou thenke of þat aray,
Certys þou schalt not synne!
(*homo memento finis et in eternum non peccabis*)

MALUS ANGELUS

ȝa, on þi sowle þou schalt þynke al betyme. –
Cum forth, man, and take non hede.
Cum on, and þou schalt holdyn hym inne,
þi flesch þou schalt foster and fede
Wyth lofly lyuys fode.   (407–15)

...

The verse is tight, the rhythm driving, the words short and plain. As we move between the two speeches the Good Angel's urgent "þynke ... thenke ..." is picked up immediately by the Bad Angel and tossed aside: "ȝa, on þi sowle þou schalt þynke al betyme." The effect seems quite intentional, and very effective if not broken up by the Latin quotation. To have the Good Angel speak the tag line, "*homo memento finis et in eternum non peccabis*," after the final line of his stanza seems to work directly counter to the dramatic and poetic rhythms observable in the writing at this point, and to be quite out of keeping with the playwright's normal skilful control of these aspects of his text.

Again, it seems inconceivable that a writer who so often uses the effect of a "pick-up" line to maintain a rhythmic and thematic drive between stanzas spoken by different characters, would choose deliberately to undermine this by inserting an extra-metrical line of Latin. His normal use of the technique may be seen throughout the Banns, or in the sequence of speeches by the Virtues where they discuss Mankind's desertion from the Castle:

PRIMUS VEXILLATOR

...

Glotony, and oþyr synnys boþe grete and small.
þus Mans soule is soylyd wyth synnys moo þanne seuyn.

SECUNDUS VEXILLATOR

Whanne Mans sowle is soylyd wyth synne and wyth sore,
þanne þe Goode Aungyl makyth mykyl mornynge
...   (38–41)

CARITAS

...

For if he wyl to foly flyt,
We may hym not wythsyt. –
He is of age and can hys wyt,
Be knowe wel euerychon!

ABSTINENCIA

Ichon, ȝe knowyn he is a fole,
In Coueytyse to dyth hys dede.   (2592–97)
...

The same technique may be seen in this passage early in the play between Folly and Lust-liking, but this time apparently totally undercut by a Latin gloss so that the effect is lost:

VOLUPTAS

...
Whoso wyl wyth þe Werld haue hys dwellynge,
And ben a lord of hys clothynge,
He muste nedys, ouyr al þynge,
Euermoer be couetowse!
(*Non est in mundo diues qui dicit 'habundo'.*)

STULTICIA

3a, Couetouse he muste be,
And me, Foly, muste haue in mende!   (500–505)

In the manuscript, the Latin is written in the scribe's normal hand following the last line of the stanza proper, and is itself followed by the rule which separates the two stanzas. Despite its physical claim to be considered part of the play-text, however, the authenticity of the line must again be questioned. The verbal rhythm, and the dramatic effect of the carry-over between the two speeches – "He muste ... be couetowse/ 3a, couetouse he muste be" – would be lost completely if the Latin were accepted as being part of the spoken text. This loss is, in fact, not nearly so apparent if one is simply reading the text silently on the page. As the eye scans automatically ahead, the mind perceives the verbal patterning clearly. Despite the presence of the Latin tag sandwiched between the lines in question, the reader is able to appreciate the aesthetic effect of the verbal bridge the playwright has created between the two speeches. Not so the listener. For the audience at a performance who only hear the lines through once and cannot scan visually back and forth, or even for the reader who reads the lines through aloud, the experience is entirely different. Now if the Latin line is spoken between the speeches, the carefully patterned connection created by the carry-over lines is lost. The pattern of the carry-over is used so frequently and so strikingly elsewhere in the play, as we have noted above, that there seems no question that the playwright intended it here too. We must conclude once more, therefore, that the Latin is out of place as part of the spoken text – though of course not as part of a commentary.[37]

There are other ways, too, in which the experiences of a reader of the play-text and the audience hearing the play in live performance differ in ways crucial to our argument. In addition to the very different perceptions of verbal patterns noted above, there may be very different perceptions of meaning in the two cases. If, for instance, there is a problem with the interpretation of one of the Latin tags, as in our first two examples, the reader may pause for consideration of the scriptural or other quotation and then pass on. If the meaning or the wider implications are not clear, he can refer back to a previous part of the text or quickly scan ahead for clarification. These possibilities are not available to an audience. The medieval audience at a performance of *The Castle* would have been no more able than those in a modern audience – and no more willing – to pause for reflection on a gloss, or for thoughtful consideration of the wider implications of a Biblical or other citation, for if they had they would have lost the next few lines of the play or the next part of the action. In the case of the kind of verbal references we have been discussing, the meaning must be apprehended immediately or it will not be apprehended at all. The play in performance will not wait.

One might perhaps argue, of course, that the Latin glosses and references were only intended to be fully understood by learned members of the audience who knew Latin and would not need to pause to reflect upon the meaning of familiar quotations. The general mass of the popular audience, for whom the play seems primarily intended, would, it could be argued, simply accept the lines as "authorities". There are, however, problems which cannot be explained even by this argument.

Thus far, we gave considered examples of extra-metrical lines which appear to give problems of meaning, and others which appear to disrupt dramatic and poetic rhythm if they are allowed to stand as part of the spoken text of the play. Another kind of problem entirely may be seen in the line which is found in the right-hand margin of the manuscript at line 3521. The line is rather squeezed, and has every appearance of an addition to the page, though in the same scribal hand.[38] It reads: "*misericordia et veritas obuiauerunt sibi iusticia et pax osculate sunt*" – "Mercy and Truth have met each other; Justice and Peace have kissed." There is no question that the line is relevant to the action of the play at the conclusion of the heavenly debate, in whose context it occurs. It is, indeed, the ultimate scriptural source of the whole Four Daughters episode, and elsewhere we find the line carefully incorporated into the verse texts of both the *N-Town Parliament of Heaven*[39] and the fourth act of *Respublica*, in both of which plays the Four Daughters also appear.[40] The *N-Town* passage makes a useful comparison with that in *The Castle*:

> Misericordia
> Now is þe loveday mad of us fowre fynialy
> now may we leve in pes · as we were wonte
> Misericordia *et* veritas obviauerunt sibi
> Justicia *et* pax · osculate sunt et
>   et hic osculabunt pariter omnes[41]

The context here is somewhat different, since the debate in this case is attempting to resolve the problem of whom God shall send to earth to save man. Also, it is Mercy, and not Peace, who speaks the famous line from Psalm 85. The general dramatic features of the two passages, however, are very similar. Of the *N-Town* use of the line it may be noted that it is fully incorporated into the metrical and rhyme schemes of the verse; that it is spoken when the debate has been fully resolved;

and that it is accompanied by the appropriate action described in the stage direction given at this point.

The problem in the case of *The Castle* is that the Latin line seems to have no direct relationship whatever to the stage action, or to the verbal argument which has been going on. Peace has indeed been arguing strongly for reconciliation, and pleads:

> Lete vs foure systerys kys,
> And restore Man to blys,
> As was Godys ordenaunce! (3519–21)

The quotation from Psalms appears in the margin at this point. But the argument is, in fact, far from won. Peace has to press her case for a further twenty-six lines of verse before the reconciliation between the Daughters is apparently achieved. I say "apparently" because there is no stage direction to indicate that the Four Daughters do actually kiss. All the lines themselves reveal is that Peace stops trying to reconcile her sisters and begins to address God. Since there is no further comment by any of the other three before God himself speaks, we must assume that the reconciliation has been achieved – possibly with stage action involving the famous "kiss" – and that the debate has been resolved insofar as the Daughters are capable of resolving it. The final resolution now rests on the divine judgement.

God gives his judgement in the stanza which follows the end of Peace's speech, and from this point on there is no further contention between the Daughters. Since, therefore, God's pronouncement of mercy for Mankind is the true point at which reconciliation is achieved, it might just be argued that the "kiss" should not take place until the judgement has been given. This, however, is not the point at issue. If the playwright did intend the four to kiss as part of the stage action they may be conceived of as doing so at 3547 or 3573, but they cannot kiss at 3521, the place at which the scriptural quotation appears in the margin. The tag, on the other hand, cannot be spoken until after the kiss has taken place, for both *obuiauerunt* and *osculate sunt* indicate completed action.

One must, in the circumstances, conclude that in the position in which it occurs in the manuscript the Latin tag would actually contradict what was happening on stage at the time were it to be spoken as part of the text. Thus, it seems almost certain that the line has no place in the play-text proper. Where it does belong, and what its function actually is, are points we shall come to shortly.

Yet another ill-fitting type of tag line occurs in, or is appended to, a passage close to the end of the play, in the middle of a speech by Mercy. Significantly, the passage in question contains a good deal of Latin skilfully incorporated into the verse:

MISERICORDIA
...
Passus sub Pilato Poncio.
As þou henge on þe croys,
On hye þou madyste a voys –
Mans helthe, þe Gospel seys –
Whanne þou seydyst "Scitio!"

We then have a tag: "*Scilicet salutem animarum.*" There is some problem here with the rhythm of the verse carrying over from this stanza to the next, but none of meaning. If one understands the Latin, everything is perfectly clear. The gloss – "that is, for the salvation of souls" – is a standard medieval interpretation of the Biblical text quoted by Mercy ("*Scitio*" – "I thirst").[42] The problem, instead, is one of function: all those clerkly members of the audience who could understand the Latin of the gloss would have been familiar enough with the explanation not to need it; and the unlearned would not have understood the language and therefore could not have understood the explanation. The line thus seems to serve no dramatic or didactic function. The likelihood of its ever having been intended as part of the play text is remote.

At the outset of this paper, I argued that the six extra-metrical lines of God and the single line which begins Mercy's speech at 3313a seemed to work on a practical level, creating no acting or other production difficulties. In view of the theoretical objections I have raised to the presence of the other extra-metrical Latin lines in the spoken text of the play, I shall now turn my attention to these seven lines of God and Mercy, and attempt to examine them in terms of the same critical criteria.

First, it should be noted that all seven lines are written as if they were indeed part of the verse text. None appears in a marginal position. Second, none of the lines seems to present any problem with meaning in the context in which it is found. Third, none creates any disruption of the dramatic or poetic rhythms of the play text. One reason for this seems clear: six of the lines in question begin the stanza to which they are connected, and the stanzas seem to follow as logical developments of the thought contained in the Latin quotation. The single exception to this, God's line, "*Misericordia Domini plena est terra. Amen!*" at 3573a, appears to conclude a stanza, and is discussed separately below.

The effect achieved is very interesting. In some cases the stanzas seem like tiny vernacular sermons developing from the appropriate Latin *thema*[43]. In others, the tag is in the first person (in four out of the seven examples, in fact). In one, the initial Latin text seems to have been integrated grammatically into the vernacular lines which follow:

PATER

Sedens in iudicio
Sicut sintill(a) in medio maris,
My mercy, Mankynde, ȝeue I þe.
Cum – syt at my ryth honde!   (3597a–99)[44]

Grammatically, the line given to Mercy at 3313a would appear to function in somewhat the same way. Of even greater significance, however, is the fact that her quotation from scripture has been significantly adapted from its source in order to make it work as a personal plea. The original passage in 2 Corinthians from which the line derives reads as follows:

Benedictus Deus et Pater Domini nostri Jesu Christi, Pater misericordiarum, et Deus totius consolationis:/ Qui consolatur nos in omni tribulatione nostra: ut possimus et ipsi consolari eos, qui in omni pressura sunt, per exhortationem, qua exhortamur et ipsi a Deo.
                                      (2 Cor. 1:3–4)[45]

Only the middle part of this passage has been taken by the playwright. But he has changed the meaning completely by the addition of an "O" at the beginning, so that the passage now reads as a direct address by Mercy to God. Finally, he has left the extracted portion grammatically incomplete, apparently so that it may flow naturally, as a parenthetical statement, into the English lines which follow:

MISERICORDIA

O Pater misericordiarum, et Deus tocius consolacionis,
qui consolatur nos in omni tribulacione nostra!
O þou Fadyr, of mytys moste,

> Mercyful God in Trinite,
> I am þi dowtyr, wel þou woste,
> And mercy fro heuene þou browtyst fre.
> ...   (3313a–3317)

The Latin is neither glossed nor paraphrased in English by anything that follows in Mercy's lengthy speech.

Just as the scriptural quotation introduced here has been adapted so that it may function naturally and in a grammatically correct manner as a direct address by Mercy to God, so three of God's scriptural quotations have been chosen, apparently, so that they function naturally as lines given in the first person, as for instance here:

PATER

> *Sedens in trono*
> Ego cogito cogitaciones pacis, non affliccionis.
> Fayre falle þe, Pes, my dowtyr dere!
> On þe i þynke, and on Mercy. ...   (3560a–3562)[46]

Such adaption and choice of first person quotations seem logical reasons underlying the observed fact that the group of seven lines under discussion here work perfectly well as part of the spoken text in performance.

There remains for discussion at this point God's line at 3573a, which unlike the others in this group seems to conclude rather than begin a stanza: "*Misericordia Domini plena est terra. Amen.*" In form and content this seems to fall naturally into place as setting the final seal on the judgement God has given on Mankind's soul. It also sums up God's reasons for giving the judgement. The concluding "*Amen*" is surely proof positive that the line is part of the play-text proper. It does not appear in the scriptural source (Psalm 33:5), which is otherwise quoted verbatim, and cannot be other than a spoken line.[47]

The analysis undertaken in this paper has suggested that of the forty-six extra-metrical Latin tags found in *The Castle*, only those six found in God's speeches and the single line of Mercy noted above appear beyond reasonable doubt to be part of the play itself. The others, I have suggested, should not be regarded as belonging to the spoken text. Such a conclusion, however, leaves us with questions about what the other lines are, and why the scribe included them in the text of the play as he copied it. The discovery at some future date of a further manuscript of the play, especially a manuscript prior to the extant copy, would probably provide clear answers to these difficult questions. Barring this unlikely occurrence, the answers I will suggest here must remain conjectural and therefore inconclusive. There are, however, precedents for the marginalia problems in *The Castle* manuscript.

The gradual accretion of learned commentary to texts of all kinds from the classical period on, and the eventual inclusion of some of this commentary by scribes as part of the texts proper, is a well-known phenomenon in the manuscript transmission process.[48] I would suggest that in the case of *The Castle*, the lines in question probably represent annotations to a prior manuscript copy of the play, and that the scribe has copied them just as he found them in his original. The twenty-eight marginal tag lines appear in that position in the extant copy because that is exactly where they appeared in the manuscript from which the scribe was copying – no matter that they were in a different hand from the main body of his copy text, his aim was to reproduce what he found in front of him. The eleven other Latin tags rejected here as part of the play text proper appear in the position of stanza lines in the extant manuscript because, once more, that was where the scribe found them. They had been added as interlinear rather than marginal glosses to his copy text, or perhaps to an earlier copy still. It may indeed well be that such a combination of marginal and interlinear glosses indicates at least two separate annotators in the prior history of our extant manuscript. We cannot tell. But such a layering of manuscript accretions would certainly parallel the layering which may clearly be detected among the various stage directions and staging annotations. My own current feeling is that there are, in the manuscript, at least five distinct groups of directions and annotations regarding the staging of the play, and that each is likely originally to have been the product of a different author.[49]

The question why, if the explanation I have offered above is correct, some dozen of the marginal tag lines show greater or lesser degrees of squeezing, is a difficult one. Clearly the scribe would not have felt compelled to reproduce faithfully the squeezing which might have been exhibited by an earlier annotation. One can again only offer a conjectural explanation of the phenomenon. Most of the squeezed lines have the appearance of having been added after the main body of text on the pages in question was complete (2634a gives a very clear example of this: the tag line can only have been added in the margin after the rule had been drawn under the stanza to which it refers). Perhaps the scribe was adding a set of glosses from a second copy of the play; or, as he checked back over each page of his copy, was adding his own source glosses where they seemed appropriate. We simply cannot tell.

The *Castle* manuscript, as a whole, provides evidence of a high degree of scribal accuracy. It is, in general, remarkably free of uncorrected errors, and I would suggest gives us every reason to believe that the scribe has reproduced his original faithfully, albeit at times confusingly, for subsequent readers, directors and performers of the play. But then it may well be that while the play itself was originally written to be performed or to be read as a play, the manuscript which has survived was not. Perhaps what we now possess is a manuscript copy of the text made for a reader with quite different interests – for contemplation, for example, by one who had no theatrical or even literary interest in the text whatsoever. An argument might be made for an edition of the text which treated it in just this way. We are ourselves concerned here with the problems of editing the text we possess as a play, a theatrical entity. At the same time, the question must be asked, to what extent should an edition prepared with this end in view reflect, or at least acknowledge, the intention of the person who produced the manuscript copy we are dealing with? The question must, I think, be asked afresh before the attempt is made to edit, or re-edit any early play of this kind; and it can only be answered by reference to the kind of reader to whom a particular edition is directed.

In any edition of *The Castle* aimed at a dramatic or literary readership, the thirty-nine Latin tag lines which have been called into question in this paper have no justifiable place in the main body of the text. The primary evidence for such a conclusion has been shown to be of a very básic nature: the lines do not – and, I have argued, cannot – work in performance. When they are analysed and their content fully explored, the reasons for the unworkability become clear: if included they disrupt dramatic and poetic rhythm and often the continuity of thought itself. On occasion they even interrupt or confuse the action of the play. When the manuscript is examined in the light of these practical difficulties, paleographical considerations make it clear that a strong case can be made that the lines were originally commentary, both marginal and interlinear, and that they were never intended by their author or authors to be added to the play-text proper. It has been shown beyond a shadow of doubt that the playwright or his redactors were perfectly capable of incorporating into the dramatic verse whatever Latin they wished to use – be it scriptural texts, parts of liturgical offices, or commonplace sayings. Given the evidence presented here, there seems no reason to believe that the thirty-nine lines ever formed part of the original play text, or of any subsequent revision of the play.

I have taken pains in this paper to stress the particular contribution made by practical theatrical experimentation to the scholarly problems of editing a particular early play, but I will conclude by suggesting that this is by no means a unique example of the way in which practical theatre and scholarship may work usefully together. In medieval drama, as in any other kind of drama, the practical and the theoretical are mutually dependent. We are quite accustomed to the notion that in drama the text can only be fully realized, and therefore perhaps only fully understood, in production. We are similarly accustomed to the idea that those responsible for the performance of a play depend heavily on the perceptions of editors and textual critics who have revealed the patterns of themes, images, and verbal modes woven into the text by the playwright. We are not so accustomed to thinking of practical theatre and the editorial process by which a text is established as being similarly symbiotic. I hope this paper may have served to show that while the director almost always owes a great debt to the editor, the editor may on occasion have much to learn from the director.

Tom Stoppard remarks in his preface to his play *Jumpers* that there is really no such thing as a definitive text of a play. Statistically, thirty-nine lines may be regarded as somewhat marginal in a text of some thirty-six hundred or so. But future editors of *The Castle* would do well, I suggest, to look carefully at this margin of error for what it reveals about what the playwright intended his text to be, and for the perspective it may give us, in turn, on what we would wish our own texts to be.

NOTES

1. See the discussion below, pp 44–5 and in n 34, p 44. The tag is found at line 516a in the edition of *The Castle* included in Mark Eccles, ed., *The Macro Plays*, London, EETS OS 262, 1969. Line references throughout the paper are to this edition. For detailed study of the points raised here a more useful, though less universally accessible edition is that of David Bevington, ed., *The Macro Plays: The Castle of Perseverance; Wisdom; Mankind*, The Folger Facsimiles, Manuscript Series, vol. 1, Washington, 1972. Bevington's line numbering follows that of Eccles.
2. See below, pp 44–5 for this reference.
3. David Mackenzie Parry, "*The Castle of Perseverance*: A Critical Edition," Diss., University of Toronto, 1982.
4. August 4–6, 1979. Details of this production and visual documentation may be consulted in the archives of the *Poculi Ludique Societas* at the University of Toronto. A complete visual record of the production is also available on videotape. See D. Parry, M. Edmunds, E. Glickman, eds., *The Castle of Perseverance*, Toronto, University of Toronto Media Centre, 1980. A full check list of modern productions of the play to 1982 is to be found in Parry, Diss., pp 117–134.
5. The modernized text is in the PLS Archives, and we hope will be published.
6. This is a crucial problem for the actor as well as for the audience, since he or she must motivate the line and shape its delivery accordingly – a difficult task if the line does not fit its context. This acting problem remains even if one regards it as inessential that the audience actually understands what is being said in the Latin lines.
7. See the discussion of line 3521a below, pp 51–3.
8. 3560a, 3573a, 3597a, 3610a, 3623a, 3636a.
9. 3313a.
10. This is, of course, still a highly subjective criterion. One

can only try to be as objective as possible about the "terms" the work itself lays down: the playwright's normal stylistic patterns and approaches to structure.

11. Michael J. Kelley, "Fifteenth-Century Flamboyant Style and *The Castle of Perseverance,*" *Comparative Drama*, 6 (1972), p 24.

12. The entire manuscript is in a single hand throughout, and dates from c. 1440 (see Bevington, pp xvii – xviii). This seems to be a copy of a version of the play dating from c. 1425 which shows evidence of at least one major revision. See Parry, Diss., pp 19–27.

13. Programme in PLS Archives, University of Toronto.

14. The problem of the stage directions is dealt with at length in Parry, Diss., pp 104–117.

15. The term "author" is used here in the singular simply for convenience. See n 12 above.

16. While line references are to Eccles, my readings here and elsewhere occasionally vary from those of Eccles, as does my punctuation of the text.

17. Biblical passages and references are from the Vulgate. See *Biblia Sacra*, 4th ed., Bibliotheca de Autores Cristianos, 1965.

18. E.g. *Mankind*, ll 847–914, *Wisdom*, ll 1125–1163, in Eccles, *op. cit.*

19. See Eccles's note on l 866a.

20. Peter Happé, *Four Morality Plays*, London, 1979, p 621, n 362.

21. *The Macro Plays*, London, EETS ES 91.

22. An example is to be found in Eccles, l 3534a.

23. See Eccles, l 3547a for an example.

24. See Bevington, p xviii.

25. See n 8 above.

26. l 3313.

27. See Eccles, l 2007a for an example.

28. See Eccles, l 2638a for an example.

29. The sign is used elsewhere in the manuscript for other purposes also. See Bevington, p xxi.
30. See, e.g., 2007a, 2020a in Mankind's speech on folios 174ᵛ–175ʳ.
31. Kelley develops his idea of "flamboyant design" further in a later book, *Flamboyant Drama: A Study of The Castle of Perseverance, Mankind, and Wisdom*, Carbondale and Edwardsville, 1979.
32. Kelley, *Flamboyant Drama*, p 43.
33. The fuller passage in Proverbs, to which the gloss refers, seems to support such an interpretation quite strongly.
34. The quotation is exact. *Penes* actually takes the accusative, and though the contraction *dni* is clear enough in the manuscript, it seems likely the scribe mistook a final minim stroke for an *i* in the manuscript from which he was copying, and that the original was either *deum* or *dominum*. The gloss seems to originate from Eccles. 1:1, which accounts for the reference to "þe wysman".
35. The auspices of the play are likely to have been popular, to judge by references in the Banns.
36. See Ecclesiasticus 7:36.
37. The thought – "there is not a rich man in the world who says, 'I have enough'" – is a commonplace saying (see Eccles, p 189), and is expressed frequently in the play-text in a variety of ways.
38. At the bottom of f 189ᵛ.
39. See K.S. Block, ed., *Ludus Coventriae, or The Plaie Called Corpus Christi*, London, EETS ES 120, 1922, pp 99–104.
40. Ed. W.W.Greg, London, EETS OS 226, 1946.
41. Block, p 103.
42. John 19:28.
43. For examples, see W.O.Ross, ed., *Middle English Sermons*, London, EETS OS 209, 1940.
44. The punctuation here is rather different from that adopted by Eccles.

45. "Blessed be the God and Father of our Lord Jesus Christ, the Father of mercies and the God of all comfort:/ Who comforteth us in all our tribulation, that we may also be able to comfort them who are in all distress, by the exhortation wherewith we also are exhorted by God."

46. The tag may be translated, "I think thoughts of peace, not of afflictions" (cf. Jer. 29:11). Given by God in English in the *N-Town Parliament of Heaven* as his judgement on the Daughters' argument: "I thynke þe thoughtys of pes. and nowth of wykkydnes/ this I deme to ses ȝour contraversy." Block, *op. cit.*, pp 101, 137–138.

47. "The earth is full of the mercy of the Lord. Amen."

48. See e.g., L.D. Reynolds and N.D. Wilson, *Scribes and Scholars: A Guide to the Transmission of Greek and Latin Literature*, Oxford, 1967, esp. pp 21–22, 156–158.

49. See n 14 above.

Stage Directions and the Editing of Early English Drama

Peter Meredith

Lordinges, sovereynes, gode men and women, my paper will take the shape, and I fear possibly the tone, of a medieval sermon. "My theme is always oon and evere was," not *Radix malorum est cupiditas* (the root of this evil lies elsewhere), not *Nosce teipsum*, but *Noscete directiones theatrales vestros* – Know your stage directions! In the best tradition of medieval sermon there will be a distinct bias towards the *exemplum*, and no doubt I shall also fall into the medieval preacher's habit of arid enumeration and dogged moralising.

Noscete directiones theatrales vestros – what do we mean when we use the term "stage directions"? Consider these three examples:

> Evening in the Sierra Nevada. Rolling slopes of brown with olive trees instead of apple trees in the cultivated patches, and occasional prickly pears instead of gorse and bracken in the wilds. Higher up,

> *tall stone peaks and precipices, all handsome and distinguished. No wild nature here: rather a most aristocratic mountain landscape made by a fastidious artist-creator. No vulgar profusion of vegetation: even a touch of aridity in the frequent patches of stones: Spanish magnificence and Spanish economy everywhere.*
> ...
>
> (Shaw, *Man and Superman*, Act III)

and so on for another three and a half pages.

> *Petey.* Let him ... sleep.
>   (*Pause*)
> *Meg.* Wasn't it a lovely party last night?
> *Petey.* I wasn't there.
> *Meg.* Weren't you?
> *Petey.* I came in afterwards.
> *Meg.* Oh.
>   (*Pause*)
> It was a lovely party. I haven't laughed so much for years. We had dancing and singing. And games. You should have been there.
> *Petey.* It was good, eh?
>   (*Pause*)
> *Meg.* I was the belle of the ball.
> *Petey.* Were you?
> *Meg.* Oh yes. They all said I was.
> *Petey.* I bet you were, too.
> *Meg.* Oh it's true. I was.
>   (*Pause*)
> I know I was.
>   CURTAIN
>
> (Pinter, *The Birthday Party*, end of Act III)

Finally, and unavoidably, an example from Shakespeare:

Exit.

Any non-literary person might well be puzzled to know what the common ground is between these three diverse examples. The basic – and prosaic – answer is of course that they all come before, between or after a piece of dialogue within a play, and that they are all printed in italic. One could add to this that they do, somewhat surprisingly, have a certain similarity of style. On the grammatical level there is a tendency to ignore normal sentence structure or to depend upon a series of simple sentences. Verbs are usually in the present tense or in a curious hybrid of subjunctive and imperative; sentences are affirmative and usually declarative. Lexically they depend heavily on a limited number of frequently repeated words, though having potential access to every word in the language. The style tends to be abrupt, and the content descriptive. If you are in any doubts about the distinctive style, then consider this example of a stage direction out of its dialogue and its italics:

Puff.	Yes, sir – now she comes in stark mad in white satin.
Sneer.	Why in white satin?
Puff.	O Lord, sir – When a heroine goes mad, she always goes into white satin. – Don't she, Dangle?
Dangle.	Always – it's a rule.
Puff.	Yes – here it is. "Enter Tilburina stark mad in white satin, and her confidant stark mad in white linen."

(Sheridan, *The Critic*, Act III)

There is one of the almost inevitable words, "Enter", in its peculiar tense; the (rather cluttered) simple sentence; the description and the (relative) brevity. Curiously enough even Shaw, determined though he was to avoid the traditional "stage-directionese", could not avoid the style to some extent: the lack of subordination, the present tense, the descriptive content.

Still my non-literary enquirer might be dissatisfied with these answers. He might admit that what we call "stage directions" have a certain homogeneity of style, of context and of presentation on the page; but why, he might ask, should they be called "directions" and what have they to do with the "stage"? Let's return to my three initial examples. In the first case the answer is clear, and I am grateful to Paul Mulholland for drawing my attention to Shaw's own words on the subject:

> I made a resolution, which is still unbroken, that no play of mine, however full its stage directions, should ever mention the stage or use any technical term that could remind the reader of the theatre or destroy the imaginative illusion.[1]

Shaw's stage directions quite deliberately are not of the stage and do not direct. They are what a literate playwright can produce for a reading audience. The famous Pinter *pauses*, on the other hand, are, so I'm told, the effect of playing upon the text, suggestions deriving from actual performance. They are of the stage, and if not directions, are certainly guide-lines for delivery and timing. Both of these examples, you will notice, we can explain and discuss with some confidence because they are of our own time or from a known context. We can therefore tell why they are there and what their actual relationship is with performance: but what of the Shakespearean *Exit*? Has it, first of all, any authority? And if so, what sort? Is it to do with performance? Does it stem from the author, or is it simply something like the reflex action of a printer on reaching the end of a scene? We understand it to be a "stage direction" but despite the enormous amount of work which has been done on text and theatre, we have not got the necessary context to explain its nature. We know what it is but we do not know what, if any, is its relationship with performance. As with the Shakespearean example, so with medieval stage directions – and even more so. We recognise the thing – it has the marks of a stage direction, set apart from the text, peculiar in style, descriptive in content – but how can we know its relationship with performance? Who added it, or was it part of the author's copy? Is it, like Shaw's, a reader's aid, and, like his, inevitably catching the style? Or is it a director's memory-jogger?

Before, in this very inadequate state, we turn to the main topic of this paper, early English drama, I should like to look in some detail at a continental text that seems to provide us with just the kind of background knowledge we need to understand and interpret stage directions. Not only should this show just how limited is our English evidence but it may also provide us with some insight into the nature and style of "true" stage directions.

One of the most famous staging texts of what we (in our loose way) call the Middle Ages, relates to the performance of a Passion Play at Mons in 1501. The text of this play was borrowed from Amiens (a town about 70 miles away) and re-copied in Mons; but of this copy only the text of the third day survives. Fortunately it was largely a compilation and adaptation of the two great French Passions of Greban and Michel,[2] so that up to a point it is possible to re-create it. After the copying of the text the same scribes were set to making what were called the *abregiés*. These consist of the first and last lines of all the speeches in the play, the stage directions and the speakers' names, and are, in fact, abridgements of the text for production purposes. There were originally two *abregiés* for each of the eight days of the performance, sixteen in all. Gustave Cohen in 1925 published an edition of one complete set of *abregiés* under the title *Le Livre de Conduite du Regisseur* (something like "The director's production book") and it is to this text that I now wish to turn.[3] We know that the *abregiés* were written specifically for *this* performance of *this* Passion; here if anywhere we should be able to discover true stage directions.

The first thing that you notice about the *abregiet* is that though it is thoroughly practical in intention, it is well-written.[4] These are not hastily scribbled production notes. The text of the play is, as I have said, cut down to *incipits* and *explicits* with the rest of the speech indicated only by a number on the right to show the total length. At the first appearance of a character (and sometimes later) not only the character-name but also the name of the actor is given. Above all, the page is dominated by the stage directions; not simple exits and entrances but specific information about what is to happen, when it is to happen, and in some cases, how it is to be done. Let me take you through part of the Creation section. The first direction, immediately after the end of the Prologue, is as follows:

> *Le Ciel doit aparoir quant Dieu ara dit*: "Et que riens ne se monstre hors." *Aussi quant il dira*: "Scituons pour prendre retrait," *le feu doi(b)t aparoir, aussi l'air, l'eaue et la terre.* (Cohen p 7)
>
> (The heaven ought to appear when God says: ... Also when he says: ... the fire ought to appear, also the air, the water and the earth.)

Annoyingly this does not tell us *how* the creation of the heaven was managed nor that of the elements, but it does tell us exactly when, and reference to the Greban text helps somewhat to re-create the moment:

> *Et pour commancer nostre ouvrage,*
> *creons le ciel en hault estage*
> *d'une forme ronde esperique*
> *affin qu'il conserve et implique*
> *dedans soy tous les aultres corps*
> *et que riens ne se monstre hors.* (ll 273–8).
>
> (And to begin our work
> let us create the heaven in a high place
> in spherical form
> so that it keeps and contains
> in itself all other bodies
> and that nothing appears outside)

God has previously described his singularity and the reasons for the Creation, and he now begins the Creation itself. The heaven is followed by the elements, as spheres within it, as the Greban text makes clear (ll 279–99). This is followed by the creation of the angels; another stage direction in the *abregiet* describes this, the nine orders appearing in three groups of three (Cohen, p 7). What makes these directions convincing as evidence of staging is the very precise detail of when effects happen. Who but a director/stage manager needs to know such things? That they do not explain *how* something is done is not surprising; that is not a matter for the day of performance but the days of preparation, and a *how* in a stage direction is really a bonus.

These detailed stage directions are followed by an inexplicable gap; a series of *incipits* and *explicits* unrelieved by any directions except those attached to speakers' names:

> Lucifer, *en c(h)eant de Paradis*, ...
> ...
> Sathan, *en cheant*, ...
> ...
> Lucifer, *en Enfer* ...
> ...

(Lucifer, in falling from Paradise

Satan, in falling

Lucifer, in Hell)

and in the second *abregiet*:

[*En enffer en forme de Deable.*] (Cohen, p 8)
(In hell in Devil's form.)

For the Fall of the Angels surely something must have been happening. Why did the director not need to know?[5]

The next stage direction proper comes with God's long speech working through the rest of the creation to the creating of man:

> *Quant dieu dira*: "Nommons jour et tenebres nuit", *lors s'ap(p)ert la lumiere. Apres, le ciel nom(m)et le firmament, divisant les eaues pour la mer. Enssivant la terre appert, plaine no(m)mée; aussi herbes, arbres, pommiers et sepmences; ou firmament, le soleil et la lune et des etoilles. Eaues produisent poissons et autres reptiles; oiseaux, les ungs en mer, autres en terre. La terre produise bestiaux, oeilles, vacques, chevaulx, jumens et autres reptiles pluiseurs. Quant Dieu ara dit*: "Se deschenderons en la terre", *il descend et s'en vient au camp de Damas(c)ene. S'il est trop loing, silete. Quant il a dit*: "Sera et d'une ame informe", *il thire Adam hors: et, apres* IIII *lignes enssivant, Dieu fait samblant de aspirer sus Adam puis le prent par le main et le lieve tout droit en disant*: "Homme, or es formé pour le mieulx".
>
> (Cohen, p 9)

(When God says: ..., then the light appears. After,

the heaven called the firmament, dividing the waters to make the sea. Following that the land appears, called earth; also grass, trees, fruit trees and seed; in the firmament, the sun and the moon and stars. The waters produce fish and other creatures; birds, some in the sea, others on land. The land produces animals, sheep, cows, horses, mares and many other creatures.[6] When God has said: ..., he descends and goes to the field of Damascene. If he (it?) is too far off, music. When he has said: ..., he draws Adam out; and, after the four lines following, God pretends to breathe on Adam, then takes him by the hand and raises him upright saying: ...)

I have set this out in full so that you, as I did, will begin to have doubts. Is this really going to be much use to a director? The first direction certainly pinpoints the moment for an effect; as God speaks these words, so light appears. Well and good, but how helpful is it thereafter to be given simply a paraphrase of the text (which is all it is)? A check on what should be happening? Perhaps. Or possibly, to look at it from a different point of view, a preliminary indication of what a director needs to look out for when he approaches the text in the first place? In which case, not really a stage direction in any immediate sense.

The rest of the direction seems to be more concerned with performance; especially, "S'il est trop loing, silete." Allowing, however, for the undoubted general interest of this kind of stage direction which clearly shows the covering of movement with music, it is worth asking what it implies for this particular production. Does it for example mean that if, on the day, God *happens* to be too far away, then the director should immediately summon the musicians to play? Or does it rather mean that this is something for the director to think about in advance, and if the positioning of heaven and Adam's birthplace requires it, the musicians should play while God moves? If the latter is true, then once again we are dealing with preliminary considerations rather than immediate stage directions. I go back to my theme; take nothing on trust, *Noscete directiones theatrales vestros.*

There is another point I should like to make regarding the Mons *abregiés*. Cohen's excellent edition (and there is no doubt that it is excellent) sets out all the stage directions *between* the abbreviated speeches; yet if one looks at the single page of the original which he has reproduced in his volume (facing p xx) it is quite clear that there are a number of different positions in which the stage directions appear. I have reproduced this lay-out on p 75; all the material on that page is contained in Cohen, p 12. The first thing to notice is that only one of the directions goes right across the page and is therefore between the speeches. The others are confined to the left-hand side. Cohen has therefore had to decide where to place the left-hand ones and has chosen to place them between the speeches. This means that at least two of the directions on that page seem to come after the actions they describe – I am thinking of the giving of the name of Eve, which clearly happens within Adam's speech, and the giving of the tunics, which happens within God's. In these two cases, as it happens, the speeches are short and so the dislocation is not great, but it throws some doubt upon other places where this may happen in longer speeches but where we cannot know because we have no access to the original. Furthermore, on this page the two directions that I have just mentioned are actually joined to the centre of the two speeches by lines drawn from the direction to the text; so that there is no doubt about where they come. Access to the original, looking at the manuscript, is an important part of knowing one's stage directions.

nota	Quand Il a dit . tous les jours en mengant la terre Lors le serpent chiet sur sa poitrine Et enfin dieu sabsente deulx et sen va soubz paradis comme dessus	**Dieu** Mauuais serpent et decepuable Te faulra Retourner en fin	xxxvj
		adam O souuerain . pere diuin Tant que la mort y meth le chez	xxxviij
Nota	de en ce pas aduertir Dieu qui est desoubz la salle de paradis . de faire aporter / apres luy par deux angles quand Il Retournera en paradis terrestre / Deux plichons . que on ara prepare / pour les donner a adam et eue / –		
		Eue Je suis cause de cest exchez vous plaise vng peu considerer	viij
		adam Ha soeur Ne cessons deplorer durant le cours de no viage	
	Lors la serpent se part de paradis terrestre et sen va en enfer . tout trainant sur sa poitrine	**Le serpent** filz pier' parm' Jay bien joue mon personnaige Ne fera deable que jay fait	iiij
nota	Et se dispose dieu de venir en paradis terrestre		
	Il luy donne le nom de eue	**adam** Soeur Jay pense a nostre fait Comme mere de toute gent	iiij
		Eue Sire le nom est bel et gent fonde sur proppriete bonne	
nota	Lors dieu entre en paradis terrestre / et dit ce quil senssieult		
	Il donne les ij plichons	**Dieu** Ces deux plichons Cy Je vous donne Cest mon voeul plus ny poez estre	iiij

Lay-out of a page from the first day of the first *Abregiet*.
(cf. Cohen, Plate 1 and p 12).

One piece of evidence that I have not been able to show in my transcription is the slight variation in handwriting. On the page in question it seems to me that the handwriting of the stage direction which crosses the page is closer to that of the text than is that of the left-hand ones. I don't think that they are by different scribes but rather that they may have been written at different times. Is it possible that the text and crossing directions (if I may so call them) were written out first and the other directions later? If so this could be related to a question which Cohen raises: were the *abregiés* made specially for the production at Mons, or were they copies of the Amiens *abregiés* adapted for use at Mons? In the accounts of the play they are described as being "made" not "copied", and Cohen suggests that this might indicate that they were newly created rather than simply copied from the Amiens ones. But also in the accounts the main texts are said to be "made and copied" and there may not have been much difference between the two in the mind of the scribe.[7] Timing is also relevant here. The *abregiés* were paid for on three successive dates: May 22, May 29 and June 5. The last payment is for "having made 16 *abregiés*," so clearly by that date all were complete. That date is exactly one month before the opening of the play, and about seven weeks after the final payment for the text, *ie*:

April 19   final payment for copying of text (and actors' parts?)
May 22   first payment for *abregiés*
June 5   final payment for *abregiés*
July 5   opening of play[8]

The question needs to be asked: is that a likely time-scheme for the writing-up of production notes for the play? Would the production be fixed and therefore the final directions able to be written up by June 5? Or, to look at it from a completely different angle, is it likely that directions which derive from Amiens would be written for consideration by the director as late as May – early June for a performance in early July?

My intention is not to answer these questions here, even if I could, but to stress again that knowing the context of a stage direction is essential to an understanding of it, even in so apparently self-evident a staging text as the Mons *abregiés*. One final point needs to be made. I have said that the Mons text is largely a compilation and adaptation of Greban and Michel; it is therefore worth comparing the *abregiés* with those texts to see whether the kind of directions I have been calling staging ones also appear in them. In the Creation section one thing is striking: there is no reference to the staging of the first part of the Creation at all in Greban. Here certainly the *abregiet* stands out as a staging text. In the fall of the Angels, however, where the *abregiet* has almost nothing, Greban has: "*Icy cheent et tresbuchent les mauvais anges en enfer en fourme de deables*" (after l 426) (Here the bad angels fall and tumble into hell in the form of devils); and a few lines later: "*Icy doivent fere grant tempeste*" (after l 450) (Here they ought to make a great noise). The first of these is simply a narrative description of the action, but the second undoubtedly derives from staging. When Greban reaches the creation of Adam, his "*Icy fait home*" (after l 551) (Here he makes man) comes exactly at the spot marked by the *abregiet* for God to raise Adam out of the ground; but where the Greban direction is general the *abregiet* one is specific and detailed. Finally in the description of Lucifer's (in Greban, Sathan's) journey to the terrestrial paradise, Greban has no direction where the *abregiet* has:

> Lors s'en va Lucifer en Paradis terrestre en fourme de serpent. Et est à noter que le personnage de Lucifer ne se bruge d'Enfer, jasoit qu'il ait dit cy dessus; mais est ung aultre personnage

> *qui fait le serpent et doit aller à Eve; pour ce que Lucifer ne seroit point assez à temps mis en fourme de serpent.* (Cohen, p 10)

(Then Lucifer goes into the terrestial paradise in the form of a serpent. And it is to be observed that the person of Lucifer does not stir from hell until he has said the above; but it is another person who plays the serpent and must go to Eve; because there will not be time for Lucifer turned into a serpent (*i.e.* not time for him to change into a serpent costume?)

What does this comparison reveal? First, I think that the material in the *abregiés*, whether related to Mons or not, is very clearly related to production. Secondly, that where the two differ, the Greban text often has greater consistency (*e.g.* it includes the Fall of the Angels) but also less specificity; the stage directions are more regular but more general. I would tentatively suggest that this is what one might expect since the Greban and Michel texts are "editions" for general reading and production and not related to any particular place or time. This is not to say that they will not contain staging information; it is simply to say that that information will be that much less easy to assess, as it is further away from an actual production, and more often in the form of narrative description to keep the story clear.[9]

It is high time to turn from foreign to native *exempla*, and with the warning notes of Mons ringing in our ears let us look first at some directions in the Chester cycle. But first the manuscripts. Except for single pageants, we have here five manuscripts all dating from well after the last performance of the plays.[10] They are (and I'm sure the usual explanation is right) antiquarian copies, though I'm not so sure that we have explored just what an antiquarian would use or have a copy made for. What they were copied from is not known; possibly a civic register, possibly a collection of craft copies. As antiquarian copies of uncertain origin they would seem to be unhelpful sources of staging information, but nevertheless there are a large number of stage directions in the manuscripts, placed in the left margin (except for Harley MS 2124) or centred within the text. Here in Chester we are in a slightly different position from Mons, since though the text does not possess the guarantees of staging associations that the *abregiés* do, there is a definite connection of the text with one particular place. We are nevertheless thrown back on assessing the nature of the direction almost entirely from its content. What do we find? Let us first take one or two "centred" directions from the Noah play:

> And firste in some high place – or in the clowdes, if it may bee –
> God speaketh unto Noe standinge without the arke with all his familye.
> (Lumiansky and Mills, p 42)

First of all, is this a staging direction? In one way it quite obviously is. It doesn't say, "God speaks to Noah from heaven" but from "some high place – or in the clowdes if it may bee." That is clearly not the language of narrative description. It does not, on the other hand, look like the direction for a particular staging but rather like the suggestion of a possibility. The second question then arises: could this be used to tell us about the staging of the Noah play in Chester? If we are looking for something like certainty, then my answer would be, no. This could so easily be the author's general *desideratum* – "God must be up high somewhere ... It would be nice if there could be clouds ..." On the other hand if the author had in mind staging he had seen at Chester ... There is no way of being sure.

If we turn to another direction we are faced with a different situation; in this case the existence of two directions from different manuscripts for the same action:

> Then shall Noe shutt the windowe of the arke, and for a little space within the bordes hee shalbe scylent: and afterwarde openinge the windowe and lookinge rownde about sayinge:
> (Huntington MS 2) (Lumiansky and Mills, p 53)

> Tunc Noe claudet fenestra*m* Archae et per modicu*m* spatiu*m* infra tectum cantent psalmu*m* "Save mee, O God" et aperiens fenestra*m* *et respeciens.*
> (Harley MS 2124) (Deimling, p 58)

Both directions are marking the passage of time of the Flood; one uses silence, one a psalm, but both are staging rather than narrative. Furthermore the fact of two answers to a practical staging problem of how to indicate the passing of time, gives a sense that we are here dealing with particular staging in Chester rather than general suggestions.

An even clearer example of a true staging direction is one in which an explanation is given of *how* an effect is managed. I am thinking here of the second dove:

> Tunc emittet columbam; et erit in nave aliam columbam ferens olivam in ore, quam dimittet aliquis ex malo per funem in manibus Noe: et postea dicat Noe:
> (Lumiansky and Mills, p 464).

This can only relate to staging, and even if, as I would have to admit, we have no proof that it was used in Chester, it would be wrongheaded to reject it.

Hm	A/R	B	H
Edward Gregory	George Bellin	William Bedford	?
HUNTINGTON 2	ADDITIONAL 10305/	BODLEY 175	HARLEY 2124
1591	HARLEY 2013	1604	1607
	1592/1600		

                   Primus Rex
            Syr roy, ryall and reverent,
            Deu vous gard, omnipotent.

                  Secundus Rex
            Nos summes veneus comoplent,
               novelis de enquire.

                  Herodes
staffe   staffe   Bien soies venues, royes gent,
            Me detes tout vetere entent.

                  Tertius Rex
            Infant querenues de grand parent,
               et roy de celi et terre.

                  Herodes
            Syrs, avise you what you sayne!
            Such tydinges makes my harte vnfayne.
            I read you take those wordes agayne   sword
               for feare of velanye.
            There is none soe great that me dare gayne,
            to take my realme and to attayne
            my power, but hee shall have payne
               and punished appertlye.

            I kinge of kinges, non soe keene;
            I soueraigne syre, as well is seene;
            I tyrant that maye both take and teene
               castell, towre, and towne!
            I weld this world withouten weene;
            I beate all those unbuxone binne;
            I drive the devills all bydeene
               deepe in hell adowne.

            For I am kinge of all mankynde;
            I byd, I beate, I loose, I bynde,
            I maister the moone. Take this in mynd –
               that I am most of might.
            I am the greatest aboue degree
            that is, or was, or ever shalbe;

Hm	A/R		B	H
		the sonne yt dare not shine on me		
		and I byd him goe down.		
		Noe raigne to fall, shall none be free;		
		nor noe lord have that libertie		
		that dare abyde and I byd flee,		
		but I shall cracke his crowne.		
		Non farre nor neare that doth me nye –		
		whoe wrathes me I shall him nye;		
		for everye freake I dare defye		
		that nyll me paye ne plaese.		
		But ye be beane, I shall you beate;		
		there is noe man for you shall treate.		
		All for wrothe, see how I sweate!		
		My hart is not at ease.		
staffe	staffe	For all men may wott and see –	staffe	Baculum
		both hee and you all three –		
		that I am kinge of Gallilee,		
		whatsoever he sayes or does.		
sword	sworde	What the devell should this bee?	staffe	Gladius
		A boye, a growme of lowe degree,		
		should raygne aboue my ryalltee		
		and make mee but a goose,		Iace gladium
cast vp	Cast vpp	that ringes and raignes so riallye?	Cast vp	
		All grace and goodness I have to give.		
		There is noe prince but hee shall plye		
		to doe my hartes ease.		
	staffe and an other gowne	But now you may both here and see that I reconed vp my rialtye. I red you all be ruled by mee and found mee for to please.	staffe and a nother gowne	Baculum et toga al

Primus Rex
'Vidimus stellam eius in oriente et
venimus cum muneribus adorare eum.'

Syr, wee see the starre appeare
in the east withouten were
in a merveilouse manere,
 together as we cann praye.

Secundus Rex
Wee see never non soe cleare;
by it the waye we could lere.
But when we came to your land here
 then vanished it awaye.

Besides these centred directions there are in the Chester manuscripts some directions which are, I think, much more exciting and more unusual in that they look as though their origin was the casual jottings of a prompter/director. These are the marginal directions in the Vintners' pageant. They are placed in the left margin alongside the speeches of Herod, and consist of brief references to props, or of short, sharp directions. I have set the first few of them out on two separate pages (pp 81–2) with an indication of where they appear (and how they vary) in the different manuscripts.[11] My lay-out is misleading only in that it shows the directions of Bodley MS 175 on the right rather than the left of the text; in fact only Harley MS 2124 has them to the right. The text is that of Huntington MS 2. How do these stage directions work? If I'm right they provide an almost complete model for the playing of Herod, and incidentally of the scene. To start with, the props represent aspects of Herod's character and status: the *staff* is his symbol of royal power, of which the *gown* is a supporting symbol; the *sword* is a symbol of his maniacal destructiveness. At the moment of his first encounter with the kings he grasps his *staff* in his hand as he greets them on equal regal terms:

> Bien soies venues, royes gent,
> Me detes tout vetere entent
> (Welcome, noble kings, tell me all your intent)

In the Bodley MS this controlled regality gives way to anger almost at once as Herod seizes the *sword* in response to the Third King's naming of the child-king; but in the other manuscripts, Herod makes his vaunt without giving way totally to his anger and returns to his regality (and his *staff*) with:

> For all men may wott and see –
> both hee and you all three –

that I am kinge in Gallilee,
whatsoever he sayes or does.

Immediately after, however, he is swept up in a whirlwind of passion, snatches the *sword* and finally at: "that ringes and raignes so riallye," *flings* it into the air. At once he begins to calm down again and at: "But now you may both here and see," he is once again assuming the robes of kingship, this time in reality with the donning of *another gown*. There isn't time or space, or indeed the need, to go through the whole of this scene, since the method remains the same though there are variations in detail; but one or two further points need to be made. First I have deliberately avoided being precise about the word *cast*; I have said that he *flings* his sword into the air. I would simply remind you that you can fling your hand in the air without it leaving your body. The same ambiguity is present in *cast*. The other point to consider is where the props come from. I do not believe that Herod dodged backwards and forwards snatching up props from his throne or the wagon floor or anywhere else. Particularly I do not believe that he snatched up a gown and tried (with staff in hand perhaps?) to put it on while starting his next stanza. To me these props and especially the speed with which they change signal an assistant; and who more likely than Herod's messenger? I have quite clearly moved into the area of speculation in discussing these directions, but I can only say that they seem to demand the kind of explanation that I have given. If there are any *stage* directions in medieval English drama, these are they. Perhaps I should offer one small piece of evidence. These directions do not look like antiquarian writing-up or editorial narrative filling; they look indeed like transmission from an acting original, perhaps the craft copy. My one piece of evidence suggests just that. In the margin of the only old craft copy that survives (of the Dyers' Antichrist pageant, c. 1500) there is a *stafe* twice that was never copied into a full cycle manuscript.[12] It looks as though Antichrist had a performance style similar to Herod's – perhaps all Chester ranters did.

Next to Chester, N. Town is probably the most important of texts for its stage directions.[13] I want to look at only one, and that not an important one, and ask the questions: what has this to do with staging, and what can the manuscript tell us about its nature? The direction occurs in the first Passion Play after the fetching of the ass and its foal for the Entry into Jerusalem (Block, p 238):

> *here cryst rydyth out of þe place And he wyl .*
> *and Petyr and Johan Abydyn stylle . And at*
> *þe last when þei haue don þer prechyng þei*
> *mete with jhesu.*

I have included this direction not because of its intrinsic interest but because of what it conceals. It looks at first like a typical product of the N. Town Passion Plays, carefully detailing movement in and around the *place*. But when you think about it, what does *"And he wyl"* mean? Is the actor really being given *carte blanche* to ride out of the acting area or stay put just as his fancy takes him? What does John say at the end of his sermon (ll 276–7)?

> to þe cete-ward fast drawyth he
> me semyth he is ny at þe gate.

Supposing, on the contrary, he wasn't; that the actor playing Christ decided to stay and listen. The answer to this problem lies in the compilation of the manuscript. The leaf on which this stage direction appears has been interpolated into a quire already written. The scribe for some reason thought that it was wrong for the Entry into Jerusalem to occur without the previous episode of the fetching of the ass and foal. As this did not occur in the play as he had it before him, he decided to include the episode, inserting a new leaf to do it. Having done this, however, he discovered that he had Christ in the acting-area some sixty lines or so before he needed him there. Hence this botched job of a direction is an attempt to retrieve, or possibly to conceal, the situation. We are not dealing here with staging but with scribal matters.

Whereas Chester and N. Town are rich in stage directions, York has hardly any. What it has, however, is a wealth of civic record material to provide supporting evidence for the staging of the York play. One of the most important recent discoveries in York was that of the Mercers' indenture, containing a detailed list of the items used by the company in their pageant of Doomsday.[14] The Doomsday pageant also happens to be one of the few at York with stage directions. Moreover the indenture has what almost amounts to a stage direction embedded in it:

> A brandreth of Iren þat god sall sitte vppon
> when he sall sty vppe to heuen.

At some point in the action God must ascend to heaven on the iron seat wearing, as we have been told earlier:

> a sirke Wounded a diadem With a veserne gilted,

a shirt decorated with Christ's wounds and a gold mask with a halo. The stage directions are:

> *Hic ad sedem iudicij cum cantu angelorum*
> (after l 216)
> (Here, to the seat of Judgment with the song of angels).[15]

and:

> *Et sic facit finem, cum melodia angelorum transiens a loco ad locum.* (after the final line) (And thus he makes an end, with the melody of angels crossing from place to place).

It seems, at first, as though we must have here an excellently documented piece of stage business. Unfortunately, nothing fits. Christ's movement to the Judgment seat is apparently a *descent from* heaven, and there is no reason to suppose that the passing or crossing from place to place of the final stage direction alludes to an ascent. We are also faced here with a further problem, that of date. The date of the indenture is 1433, the date of the York Register, the official civic copy, is late 1460's or 1470's.[16] Invaluable though the indenture evidence is, we cannot be sure that it relates to the text as it has survived. So once again we are thrown back on the stage directions themselves. We know that they date from the period when the play was being performed, but all they tell us is that music was used to accompany the movements of God. I should perhaps confess that the final stage direction sounds to me distinctly literary.

One way in which the civic records of York can fill out the sparseness of the original stage directions should not be forgotten. The York manuscript contains many marginal annotations and by far the largest number of these are in the hand of John Clerke, the servant of the Common Clerk at York during the later sixteenth century.[17] One of his duties was sitting at the first station of the play with the Register, the civic copy of the play, and, as we have recently discovered, noting alterations and omissions that appeared in the course of performance. These annotations, where they take the form of stage descriptions (as opposed to directions), are invaluable information about the staging of the play in York in the sixteenth century. Most of Clerke's annotations (unfortunately, from our present point of view) relate to changes in the text, but there are a few that indicate the use of music, and just one or two that relate to stage action. Sadly, though the music references are most valuable, the staging ones are almost uniformly descriptions of actions referred to in the text. Ultimately Clerke's greatest value for staging may turn out to be his evidence for the playing of two pageants together, or "in tandem" as Richard Beadle has called it.[18] These Clerke annotations, and others like them, raise a special problem in editing, and it is to editing that I must at long last turn.

I have spent almost all my time in talking about the nature of stage directions because I wish to emphasize their complexity and their importance, and the necessity of treating them with the same respect and care that is given to the text itself. They may not be able to tell us exactly how a given play was staged in the Middle Ages, but they may be all we've got. I am not one of those that believes that a play only exists in performance, but I do very strongly believe that not to consider the staging aspect of a play's existence, not to allow it the same attention that we give to the text, is ultimately fatal to our understanding of its meaning. Because of this, and this is where the dogged moralising comes in, I would say first that anyone editing a text must include all the stage directions that are present in the original text and must not add any modern ones. If you add, you not only run the risk, as David Bevington has said (see above, p 31), of your readers not noticing the difference between the old and new, but you also confuse what the original directions can reveal about the staging. Besides which, people will not take stage directions seriously if they feel that they are the kind of thing that can be made up at will. Secondly, we know far too little about the details of the staging of any single play for us to risk adding stage directions of our own. If you have ideas about the staging, or if a particular tricky piece of stage action or business needs comment, then the place for discussion is in the Introduction. Do not clutter up the text with what tomorrow may be outdated theories. Thirdly, and my whole paper has been an attempt to lead up to this, let us try to investigate and discuss the nature of stage directions with the same devotion and subtlety that we would bring to an examination of the text. They are not self-evident truths, perspicuous evidence that any fool can interpret; they are complex, many-layered, often intractable lumps of ore, and they need, and deserve, a lot of refining. Date is just one problem. Usually we don't know when a stage direction was written into the text. Sometimes, no doubt, they are original to the composition of it, often certainly they have been added. As a rule all we can do is to be aware of the possibilities. Sometimes, of course, we do know, as with John Clerke, that the directions were added later. In my opinion these "directions" should go into the text, but only if some typeface or attached reference symbol can show their date and source. Our usual problem is not when were they written, however, but *what* are they? Authors' imaginings? Preparatory thoughts? Performance notes? Readers' aids? Whatever they may be the one certain thing is that they need investigating. We need to investigate the manuscript: where are the stage directions placed on the page? Are they in various positions? Are they placed at the point where the action takes place, or are they warning directions placed earlier? If there is more than one manuscript, what variations are there? We must investigate the language: Latin, English, French? What tenses are used? We must investigate the external evidence, and above all we must investigate the content of the directions.[19] When there is no outside aid, it can sometimes help to categorize stage directions by the kind of information that they provide, as a first step towards investigating their nature. To use a typical medieval preacher's style: That, What and How. Do they tell us *That* something happened; *What* has happened; or *How* it was done? "Exit";

"Exit pursued by a bear"; "Exit pursued by a bear; it is necessary that someone be transformed into the likeness of a bear..."

Finally, every sermon should end with a prayer. My first petition would be for understanding – what was really going on in Mons in 1501? Was the Chester Herod really a juggler? What *was* the N.Town scribe trying to do? When *did* the Mercers' God "sty vppe to heuen"? My second would be on behalf of editors, that they may be allowed the space to discuss their stage directions fully, and the autonomy to refuse to mix the pure ore of original stage directions with the dross of modern additions.

NOTES

1. The letter which appeared in TLS, 25 October 1917, will be published in *Agitations: Letters to the Press 1875– 1950, Bernard Shaw*, ed. Dan H. Laurence and James M. Rambeau (forthcoming).
2. *Le Mystère de la Passion d'Arnould Greban*, ed. Gaston Paris and Gaston Raynaud, Paris, 1878; Jean Michel, *Le Mystère de la Passion* (Angers 1486), ed. Omer Jodogne, Gembloux, 1959. All references are to these editions.
3. Gustave Cohen, *Le Livre de Conduite du Regisseur et le Compte des Dépenses pour le Mystère de la Passion joué à Mons en 1501*, Paris, 1925. As the title suggests the book contains not only the *abregiés* but also the accounts of the play. It has an excellent introduction describing the manuscripts and the production of the play. It is here referred to as "Cohen".
4. Cohen provides a reproduction of one page of an *abregiet* facing p xx of his Introduction. I have transcribed this on p 75.
5. I have referred to the director throughout, but it should not be forgotten that the *conducteur de secretz* or *fainctier*, the man or men who looked after the special effects, may also have had some overall control. At Mons these were Guillaume Delechiere and his brother Jehan, brought over from Chauny a town almost as far from Mons as Amiens is. None of their "books of the play", if they had any, has survived, unless the second set of *abregiés* was intended for them. It seems that certain of the "stage staff" at Mons had "cue sheets" (*billets de advertence*), see Cohen, p 169. The absence of information about the Fall of the Angels remains a puzzle; Maistre Jehan du Fayt was paid for work on the *secret du trebuchement des Angeles* ("device for the fall of the Angels"), see Cohen, pp 559–60.
6. Some of my translations need comment. I have assumed that *plaine* in *plaine nommee* means "dry land, earth", and

that *pommiers* means "fruit trees" generally rather than "apple trees". I have translated *sepmence* as "seed" since this seems to be its meaning in Greban (l 500) and the *abregiet* seems to be here a straightforward paraphrase of this section of the text, though I can't see how it can have been a very noticeable part of the Creation. "Fruit", perhaps? The *reptiles* of the *abregiet* are the *reptile* and *reptilia* of Genesis 1, xx and xxiv, the "moving/creeping things" of the English Bibles. I have used "creatures" for both those of the water and those of the land. It could be that some specific "creeping creatures" were intended but there is no sign of this in Greban's text.

7. For Cohen's remarks see pp xxxvi – vii. The references in the accounts appear on pp 499 (*d'avoir fair xvi Abregiés*) and 482 (*a faire et recopier*). It is true, however, that the payment relating to the main texts is concerned with the paper used, whereas that relating to the *abregiés* is for the writing. Related to this question of the origin of the *abregiet* text is the treatment of the prologues. There is a separate volume of prologues for the Mons production. In one of these, reproduced in Cohen, the text of the prologue applies to the Mons production (p 459) – necessarily since this is the text spoken at Mons – but the *abregiet* text retains the references to the Amiens production (p 35). It is also worth noting that the titles of the *abregiés* also retain references to the Amiens production where the play was performed over *four* days (two sections a day) rather than eight; eg *Abregiet du Livre original de le apres diner du premier jour, dont on fait la seconde Journee* (Cohen, p xxvi, 3e cahier). In both cases, of course, the references could simply be a result of using the Amiens text of the play.

8. The references in the accounts are as follows: April 19, pp 474–5; May 22, p 489; June 5, p 499.

9. Cohen more satisfactorily compares the *abregiet* for day 3 with the text for that day which has survived from Mons. He finds the *abregiet* directions "plus nombreuses et plus précises"

(p xxxvi). I was unfortunately unable to consult the edition of this text which Cohen published. It would be wrong to suggest that the Greban and Michel texts have no staging value; see for example the seating plan for the Last Supper in Michel (p 266) or the Transfiguration (p 125) where the Michel direction has as much information as the *abregiet*.

10. The fullest and most recent discussion of the text of the Chester cycle is contained in R.M. Lumiansky and David Mills, *The Chester Mystery Cycle, Essays and Documents*, Chapel Hill, 1983, pp 3–86. The manuscripts are described in the introduction to *The Chester Mystery Cycle*, ed. Lumiansky and Mills, EETS SS 3, London, 1974, pp ix – xxvii. Three of the manuscripts have been published in the *Leeds Texts and Monographs*, Medieval Drama Facsimile Series, I (Bodley MS 175), VI (Huntington MS 2) and VIII (Harley MS 2124). A description of the stage directions by David Mills appears in METH 3 (1981) pp 45–51. Huntington MS 2 is used for the edition of Lumiansky and Mills, and Harley MS 2124 for the earlier EETS edition by Hermann Deimling (vol. I) and Dr. Matthews (vol. II), EETS ES 62 and 115, London, 1892 and 1916.

11. The text appears in Lumiansky and Mills, pp 163–5.

12. See Lumiansky and Mills, pp 505 and 508.

13. All references are to *Ludus Coventriae*, ed. K.S. Block, EETS ES 120, London, 1922. A full discussion of the manuscript is contained in Miss Block's introduction and in the introduction to the facsimile in the LTM series, IV, ed. Peter Meredith and Stanley J. Kahrl.

14. The indenture is printed in REED: *York* eds. Alexandra F. Johnston and Margaret Rogerson, Toronto, 1979, pp 55–6. Its relation with production is discussed in Johnston and Dorrell, "The York Mercers and their Pageant of Doomsday, 1433–1526," *Leeds Studies in English*, ns 6 (1972), pp 10–35; Peter Meredith, " 'Item for a grone – iijd' – records and performance," in *Proceedings of the First Colloquium, REED*, ed. JoAnna Dutka, Toronto, 1979, p 46.

15. All references are to *The York Plays*, ed. Richard Beadle, York Medieval Texts, London, 1982.

16. For the dating of the York Register see Richard Beadle and Péter Meredith, "Further External Evidence for Dating the York Register (BL Additional MS 35290)," *LSE* ns 11 (1980 for 1979), pp 51–8.

17. For John Clerke see Peter Meredith, "John Clerke's Hand in the York Register," *LSE* ns 12 (1981 for 1980 and 1981), pp 245–71. Clerke's annotations are listed and discussed in the introduction to the *LTM* facsimile of the York Play, VII, ed. Richard Beadle and Peter Meredith, pp xxi – xxiii and xxxiii – xl.

18. In the notes to pageant XV (p 428) of his edition. The principle is discussed also in the notes to pageants III and IV, and XVI.

19. A survey of the extant medieval English plays was begun at the meeting of *Medieval English Theatre* on stage directions at Westfield College, London, in 1981.

"this hawthorn-brake our tiring-house": Records of Early English Drama and Modern Play-texts.

J.A.B. Somerset

A sub-subtitle for this paper, which is concerned with the value for editors of records which survive from places for which there are no texts, might be "a survey, with a few suggestions." I have chosen my main title from the Elizabethan drama rather than from its predecessor, because I believe that recent editors of Elizabethan texts have a great deal to offer us by way of methods and approach when we edit dramatic texts which come from the period before the permanent theatres of London. I say "recent" editors because there have been advances in methodology over the last twenty years or so which are reflected, among other places, in the changing editorial policies of the New Arden Shakespeare. It seems to me that our enhanced awareness of the conditions of Elizabethan performance, brought about by the patient labours of theatre historians, has led editors, in turn, to an increased respect for texts as theatrical scripts.

Two familiar Shakespearean examples will illustrate. We

are no longer likely to have Romeo's continuing presence on stage during Mercutio's conjuration (II, i and ii) explained as theatrical clumsiness, or else edited out of the text by including superfluous exits and entrances for Romeo. Instead, the stage is accepted as being a "neutral" space with multiple possibilities; one moment it is the street with an adjacent wall, and a few moments later it is redefined as the Capulets' orchard through the speeches of the characters. Second, the scenes which alternate between Egyptian and Roman camps in the fourth act of *Antony and Cleopatra*, although still followed in recent editions (such is the conservatism of editors) because of the need to make texts agree with concordances and traditional line-numbering, are usually presented to the reader as a continuous action, fluid and tense, leading to the climactic result of Egyptian defeat. Other welcome innovations in recent Shakespeare texts are the lack of indications of "place" (which have been banished to the notes), and an increased respect for the stage-directions in the original. We are freeing ourselves from eighteenth- and nineteenth-century theatrical preconceptions. While I could mention several recent editions here, it is a pleasure to be able to single out Professor Bevington's edition of *The Complete Works*, in which all of these editorial procedures are followed. The result, for student or reader, is freedom to read with imagination and with attention to the clues offered by the lines themselves; my title is an example of a line rich in suggestions about the players' approach to their texts and their craft.

However, my focus today is upon the two-hundred-odd plays that comprise "medieval" drama and their editions, and I begin by assuming that in using the word "editions" we are speaking about edited texts in the full sense, presenting accurate texts accompanied by introductions, commentaries, and notes aimed at accounting for the textual history of the manuscript or printed copy-text which underlies the edition, outlining whatever can be gleaned about the theatrical history and nature of the play(s), and sharing the meaning of the text with readers. As Anne Hudson observed at the 1976 meeting of this conference:

> The old reductive view of the editor [of medieval texts] then – the view that the editor "merely" provides a text which the literary critic may interpret, the historian plunder, and the philologist gut for interesting forms – has to go...even at a simple level...this type of edition will not suffice.[1]

With a few exceptions, we are currently dependent upon texts a century old or older whose editors were interested in a more limited range of things than we are today. There then existed no interest in performance of the plays (censorship would have made it impossible anyway). Introductions generally limited themselves to describing the manuscripts, indicating whatever was known about the history of ownership, and attempting to date and locate them through attention to stanza forms, handwritings, dialect words, and the like. The usefulness of the texts for the *New English Dictionary* is obviously in editors' minds. Often there is attention to pronunciation through a study of rhyme words, and the question of borrowings from other plays or cycles is sometimes raised. Editors had, of course, problems over simple things like access to manuscripts – such a one may lie behind Furnivall's exasperated note to Halliwell-Phillipps in 1866: "...If Lord Ashburnham – may he soon be strangled – is not the owner of the York miracle plays, please tell me who is..."[2] But when all is said and done, many of these editors betray little consciousness that they are dealing with dramatic literature at all. When some commentary on the dramaturgy or staging is offered, it is usually perfunctory and may be accompanied by brief extracts drawn from Sharp's *Dissertation* or Archdeacon Rogers's *Breviary*. The page and a quarter of commentary on effective stage presentation in K.S. Block's edition of N-Town is unusual in its attention to such matters as "command of stage effect, and understanding of the impressiveness of significant gesture and movement."[3] But she offers no specific details, and the account is disappointingly brief.

Furnivall's introduction to *The Digby Plays* is a perhaps more typical example. His approach is condescending, since he sees the plays as relics of a Romish past and as having little or no literary merit. As regards staging, he assumes that for the *Conversion of St. Paul* and *Mary Magdalene* there must have been a pageant wagon, and that the plays were originally parts of larger lost works which were cyclical in form. After admitting that he cannot imagine how the scenic effects in the *Mary Magdalene* were managed, he concludes: "But make-believe will do wonders."[4] In assuming that there was a pageant-wagon, Furnivall betrays a tendency to oversimplify by supposing that there was a single method of staging used nearly everywhere in England, divergences from which are inexplicable or the result of local simplicity (he implies that a play not requiring a wagon-stage must be even cruder than the norm).

Aside from legitimate questions about the accuracy of their editorial work, such attitudes and procedures among early editors affected the texts being presented, sometimes in quite serious ways. I speak of the disregard for the theatrical origin and purpose of the texts, and of the various kinds of drama which they preserve. It is unnecessary to go into details here, because I can refer you to Professor Ian Lancashire's spirited survey of previous editing, in his paper to the 1976 conference.[5] One can point to the ways editors explained textual revisions in ways which ignored the theatricality of the texts; here we can contrast the attitudes of Hardin Craig and R.W. Ingram to the Coventry reviser, Robert Crow. Because his attention is on the literary quality of the lines, Craig censures him as a bad poet; on the other hand Professor Ingram stresses

Crow's dramaturgy, and presents all the facts about the two or three men who bore that name at Coventry in the sixteenth century.[6]

A comment is also in order about the excision of passages of music. Lucy Toulmin Smith excluded musical notation from her text of York play XLVI (supplying an imperfect transcription of three settings, and a facsimile of the others in an appendix), and Hardin Craig excluded it altogether from his 1902 text of the Coventry Weaver's play in spite of the fact that Thomas Sharp included it in his text of 1825. Both excisions are regrettable because the records indicate that the guilds in question lavished considerable expense on music for their pageants.[7] The York music, as John Stevens reminds us in Richard Beadle's new edition, is "unique in the surviving medieval drama";[8] in that edition, however, I am not altogether happy to find only a modern transcription of the notation (however authoritative it is) located in an appendix.

Some fairly recent decisions by the Early English Text Society have preserved older editorial practices for another generation of readers. The Craig edition of *Two Coventry Corpus Christi Plays* has been reprinted and (a fact noted by several reviewers) the new editions of *The Macro Plays* and *Non-cycle Plays and Fragments* present admirably accurate texts but without accompanying editorial materials (necessary stage-directions and explanations of staging) to explain their nature as plays. This is especially regrettable in the case of *The Castle of Perseverance*, now that the records are available from the likely environs of the play. However, let us concentrate on the present situation and future directions. Professor Lancashire's paper summed up the situation in 1976, suggested some new editorial aims, and outlined the then new-born REED project. What has happened since then, and how has our sense of the editorial task changed?

Since 1976 considerable effort has been devoted both to performances (showing that medieval drama is eminently actable) and to the records (showing that it was produced with expense and care). Of course, Records of Early English Drama is not alone responsible for salvation, nor have there lacked recent editors who have improved upon earlier efforts without ever scanning a REED edition. There remains much to be done – as Martin Stevens reminds us, for example, there has not been a fresh edition of the *Towneley Plays* since 1836[9] –and as recent reviews of editions show, there is some feeling that editorial standards are not perfect. I think there are fruitful linkages between records editing and textual editing – REED's results can materially aid future editors of texts. One way is directly – the records of a city are vital to understanding (and hence to editing intelligently) the dramatic manuscripts identified with that city. Efforts in this direction began, really, in 1935, with F.M. Salter's *The Trial and Flagellation, with other Studies in the Chester Cycle,*[10] and they have been carried forward vigorously in the last decade with the welcome appearances of new editions of the York and Chester cycles. This is the subject of Professor Johnston's paper. But if such direct linkages were to be the sum total of REED's value for editors, then the project would virtually have fulfilled its mission as far as editors are concerned. The extant drama definitely assignable to specific localities is limited in extent (the York and Chester cycle plays, and the Coventry, Newcastle and Norwich fragments); it is already served by REED editions. If one were to add the Cornish plays to the list (on grounds that they are assignable to a county), the point still holds, because the Cornish records are in active preparation.

There are some possible assignments of plays to localities; briefly to review them reminds us how complicated are the editorial problems which face us. We might, on the evidence put forward by Professor John Coldewey, include Chelmsford in the above list as an assignable home for the Digby *Conversion of St. Paul* and *Mary Magdalene.*[11] However, since Chelmsford was not in any case the original home of the plays, the texts illuminate the records as much as the records might do the texts; they show what local townspeople and a professional "property player" might have done faced with the demands of a text originally not written with local circumstances in mind, when the decision was taken to mount a special performance in 1562. If Professor Coldewey is right, the Chelmsford records are of great interest as recording a local response to this problem. We await the REED: *Essex* volume with great anticipation; at this moment this intriguing ascription remains as probable (if like me you find it convincing) or at least possible. In the cases of the assignments of the Towneley plays to Wakefield, or the N-town cycle to Lincoln, ascriptions are complicated by the existence of multiple "layers" of composition in the MSS, whereby plays written at different times and for different types of performance are found together. For N-town, the case is horrendously complex: the recent facsimile edition of the manuscript by Peter Meredith and Stanley J. Kahrl recounts the baffling details about papers, inks, and handwritings in the compilation.[12] As is the case with modern editions of *Hamlet*, we study in the texts of N-town and Towneley, versions of plays which were never performed in the manner which the "compiled" manuscripts present to the reader.

II

Although confident identifications of the homes of extant plays are few, the work of assembling and editing records goes forward. Through the efforts of the Malone Society collection of provincial records, and the first nine REED collections, the bulk of the published records already looms larger than the corpus of the drama, and by the close of REED's operations there will be many more shelf-feet of records than shelf-feet of plays. The records, of course, serve many other purposes than editorial ones. However, we may well ask, how can dramatic records from places whence texts do not survive assist the process of editing plays written elsewhere? The timing of the enquiry is appropriate, since the first two REED volumes so describable (Newcastle and Coventry) have recently appeared to join the volumes of Malone Society *Collections* containing records from Lincolnshire, and Norfolk and Suffolk. (I omit Giles Dawson's Kent volume because of his exclusion of all but a selection of records concerning local plays.) The question I raise is one which every records editor surely thinks about during the long months of toil which go into the assembling of records for a volume. Without necessarily pitying the textless editors' lot, we may glance at the nature of editing records for which there are no surviving texts, and assess the sorts of general questions the records raise which have a bearing on textual problems: in short, what is the evolution of a records editor?

From among a welter of seemingly irrelevant rubbish, the records searcher finds the occasional brief entry, and an even rarer extended or detailed account. Records generally exhibit disappointing brevity, and wearying repetitiveness whatever may be the preoccupations of the local chamberlains (waits' houses, the taking out and returning to storage of the pageant house, or what have you).[13] An impression is gained of the perfunctory nature of financial record-keeping, and of the unchanging course of life in medieval boroughs. What was "accustomed and necessary", as the Coventry scribe put it, needed not to be included in every year's accounts. Another reason for brevity is, I think, gained from the Shrewsbury records, where on several occasions one finds the scribe making up a blank set of payment and receipt records (presumably when he had not much else to do), with the amounts to be filled in at the end of the year near Michaelmas. The scribe obviously expected life to go on as usual. One also gains a sense of the insufficiency of records (given that they survive at all). For example, when at Bungay in 1570 a payment is recorded of threepence "for a paier of gloves for the wyttche,"[14] one is tantalized (but perhaps not enlightened) by this unique reference in a broken collection spanning nearly 200 years. Similarly, at Shrewsbury in 1582, the lavish entertainments given to and by the Lord President at his keeping of St. George's Day in the town are known from an eyewitness account in a contemporary chronicle, but they are given only a line or two in the bailiffs' accounts. Things do not look promising.

The editor has to judge how to regard the extended accounts which are discovered (albeit, alas, rarely); do they detail the unusual, or merely, by a lucky break, record and corroborate normal events in greater detail? We may safely assume, in every case, that where a total is presented in a final accounting, there must have been bills, particulars, and lists from which to compile it.[15] The question is why such materials are sometimes incorporated into the final accounts or preserved along with them. Scribal habits, or the nature of the event can give a clue. The list of properties which survives at Shrewsbury from 1525–26 is probably an example of a singular occurrence; the play that year was a special event, a performance of a play of St. Katherine in the quarry outside the walls. Of course, such a document might be preserved by accident; but it seems more likely that the scribe thought it might be useful in explaining to the auditors a singular and strange entry in his books, much in the way that we preserve receipts for the tax man. On the other hand, the entries in the churchwardens' books of Holy Trinity Church, Bungay, between 1558 and 1568, which detail payments and receipts at "the church ale & game" strike one as a lavish record of a normal (and important) event in the church year; the scribe was, happily, of a locquacious nature. Each record must, then, be assessed in its total context. The editor should, after considering both the regular and the singular recorded activities in a locality, be able to write with confidence about the "set" of records, and to produce a coherent picture of a borough's records in general, its social milieu, and its drama. I must remark in passing that I think records volumes should provide more scope for such matters to be discussed within introductions, because only the editor who has seen the records can impart the necessary sense of the context, meaning and importance of the scattered and fragmentary bits of information which are presented in the final volume.

Records editors, of course, are only human, and in their brief moments of relaxation they are apt to divert themselves by reading the published results of other records editors or by attending conferences (like this one) to share their results. Thus different places, it becomes clear, have records which illuminate each other. For example, Professor Larry Clopper's conclusion that the Chester plays as we have them are the product of extensive revision and elaboration about 1520 might have received support had the records of Shrewsbury been available; that relatively nearby borough was, for a period in the 1440's and 1450's, making quarterly payments for the eleemosynary relief of Chester's poverty. A large cycle would have been unlikely in such circumstances. Similarly (a fact rued by both myself and Professor R.W. Ingram), the Shrewsbury records can shed light upon the fortunes of the Coventry Corpus Christi celebrations, because the ordinances of the Shrewsbury Mercers' company forbade the combrethren from deserting their procession in favour of visiting Coventry. The accounts of the company regularly record fines levied upon absconders, and such may be, for given years, the only evidence about Coventry which survives. These boroughs did not live in mutually exclusive vacuums; indeed, the evidence from many parts of the country which indicates that dramatic performances were widely announced in surrounding towns, villages and cities, shows that their lives were much more interdependent than we often seem to guess, and the records of one place often directly bear upon activities in another.

Aside from direct connections, analogies between localities can be helpful. Records of revisions to a cycle such as Coventry's can shed light upon the observable revisions in surviving MSS from York, Wakefield, and Chester – the whole question of revisions awaits a full study, comparing records and texts from everywhere in a chronological matrix. Again, dramatic texts from Lincolnshire, Norfolk and Suffolk need to be carefully considered in relation to the array of county records presented in the Malone Society *Collections* volumes. The frequency there of town "games", sometimes in connection with church ales, is remarkable as is the way that the players travelled about the countryside, within limited areas, to visit neighbouring towns. It is surely more than coincidental that the great majority of travelling local plays comes from East Anglia (such as *Mankind*, the Croxton *Play of the Sacrament*, and *The Castle of Perseverance*). Editions of these plays should profit from rigorous editorial examination of the records, an examination which has only just become possible. Another similarity within a given area is the prevalence of Robin Hood plays and games in the area south of the Thames; a final one close to home for me is the Abbot of Mardol, Marham, or Marall who performed a number of times at borough expense in Shrewsbury between 1520 and 1545. What this ceremony or play may have been is suggested by a Star Chamber case from Willenhall, Staffordshire, which describes the Abbot's game as a type of King ale or King game, with contributions solicited from the onlookers (as in *Mankind*).

Besides analogies, study of the records of other areas gives rise to a sense of the uniqueness of particular localities and manners of play-making, as well as of the careful planning which went into the production of plays here, there, and everywhere. In sum, the vocation and the recreation of the records editor should serve to enhance respect for the plays as scripts, and should widen one's repertory of possible performance techniques.

At this point, the records editor is equipped to become a text editor. To put that another way, a text editor must, in my view, undergo as much as possible of the process I have just described; he or she needs to examine all available printed records (especially those from the presumed region of the play(s) under consideration) and to apply the knowledge thus gained to the manuscript or copy-text. The knowledge will be indirect, circumstantial, but nonetheless valuable, and it can aid the interpretation of the internal textual evidence and the presentation of the necessary accompanying commentary and notes.

On this question, whereas I agree with Peter Meredith's point that the texts should be kept as "clean" as possible, with editorial interventions limited to necessary emendations of corruptions, I believe that editors should exercise more latitude in their notes, pointing out the need for stage-actions (entrances, exits, and the like) and drawing upon records which outline analogous stage-practices in order to suggest how particular sequences might have been staged. For example, a note to the stage-direction in the Digby *Mary Magdalene* which calls for the burning of the temple might refer the reader to the Drapers' accounts from Coventry, which regularly record payments concerned with the final earthquake and burning of the world. Of course, one cannot assert that Coventry provides proof of how the Digby effect was managed, but until better evidence becomes available, why not present it as a possibility?

Thus to present collateral evidence about staging would remind the reader, at least, of the kind of care in staging which might have been expected. Among some modern producers of medieval plays has grown an assumption (heavily indebted to Bertold Brecht's theories of "alienation") that the observable lack of expectation of realism in medieval plays implies that audiences watched with a sense of "make-believe" which excused any effect, no matter how simple, as "theatrical".[16]

This must be placed against reminders of the lengths to which producers would go for a splendid effect. Make-believe may do wonders, but many pains were taken to present wonders anyway. In their introductions, editors are in a better position than ever before thus to discuss civic religious plays and their theatres; I do not believe that they need to abandon this wholly to the writers of monographs on the subject.

Inferences gained from a wide survey of the records can also bear upon the treatment of texts; to show how, we may ask what we want of an edition? In answer, I revert to the analogy with Elizabethan texts which began this paper. In this century we have witnessed a flood of theories, applications and practice which has been dedicated to investigating kinds of manuscripts (fair copies, foul papers, authorial drafts, prompt-copies, and the like). We do not often enough remind ourselves how much these worthy activities owe to our knowledge of play-house practices, gained from records. Another area of bibliographical investigation into the nature of the processes which produced the printed copy (through running-title analysis, compositorial analysis, and so on) depends upon a knowledge of printing-houses, whose records are gleaned as we glean those from local boroughs.[17]

An example of how our knowledge of dramatic practices can aid the presentation of editions is the treatment of cast-lists on title pages "offered for acting." The usual explanation of incorrect versions of cast-lists is that they represent fraudulent attempts to make the texts attractive to professional troupes.[18] It might, however, be possible to take this further by examining such texts carefully for internal evidence of revisions, in the light of our growing knowledge of how adaptable the troupes had to be as regards playing places, numbers of members, acceptability of texts, and the like. Evidence about revisions in texts of early interludes is, of course, readily forthcoming. REED's brief extends to 1642, and I note that provincial records from the later period have been making an impact

108 / SOMERSET

upon views of some texts. Evidence about the conditions of Elizabethan travelling players increasingly suggests that they were not all the scurvy rogues and vagabonds depicted in some early attacks on the players; in turn this is bringing about a re-assessment of relationships between troupes and texts, and the complicated questions of plays "cut for travelling". Our new insights as to how plays were acted, once again, can affect our editorial treatment of their surviving exemplars.

To return to my main theme, the ultimate goal of an editor of Elizabethan dramatic texts (from manuscripts or printed copies) is to produce editions which are scrupulously accurate and which afford a clear sense of the textual history, and hence also the *dramatic* history, of the exemplars from which they are printed. Surely this is the aim for the editor of "early" English drama as well.[19] In the most vexed cases, manuscripts, the editor needs to give a clear sense of what the scribes made of the pages they were copying or amending, and of what the relationships are between multiple-texts-within-a-single-text, and "layers of composition" within a text written at different periods. From whatever records provide collateral evidence, the editor has to keep in mind the nature of the play and its theatre, within its historical context, when discussing the nature of the manuscript or the early edition.

An example will make my point clear. The municipal "registers" of Chester and York are texts of a particular kind, and we expect to find them filled with subsequent layers of revision, interpolation, and comment. The records at York point to regular yearly performance – in fact the guilds depended upon it, since many of them began preparing very early in the year before "official" notification, collecting pageant-silver or fines in expectation of a performance.

Perusal of records from elsewhere provides many instances of a type of play which was far more prevalent in England: the saint play, found in all parts of the country, often produced with much care and expense. Since only one Cornish and two English examples survive, it has been not implausibly suggested that official displeasure at the veneration of relics and saints forced cessation of playing, and wrought the destruction of manuscripts. While saint plays quickly ceased to be acted, there are few records of such direct interference (the letter from Henry VIII to the Justices of the Peace at York in 1535 may be a forgery, and in any event it may concern the Pageant of Doubting Thomas, rather than an interlude).[20]

From reading the records one gains a clear sense of another common element among these saint plays, which may account for our lack of texts – they were "occasional" efforts, produced in the vast majority of cases only once. One possible exception, Canterbury's pageant of St. Thomas à Becket probably was, at all appearances save its last, a mechanical contrivance requiring no actors.[21] The records of Lincoln contain references, between 1441–2 and 1455–6, to five saint plays. During that period the city devoted its dramatic talents exclusively to the genre; however, each play was given in only one year. Shrewsbury provides another example. While one finds that the Abbot of Marham or Mardol (whether ceremony, game, or play) is produced fairly regularly between 1520 and 1545, the records also refer to a series of civic religious plays from 1445 to 1570, and whatever title is found occurs only once. At Bungay, the aforementioned records of the town "game" in 1558, 1567 and 1568 include payments for paper and/or for copying the parts, suggesting that new plays were being introduced. The disappearance of scripts, then, is not altogether surprising; since medieval corporations were not in the business of preserving theatrical archives, the texts were likely simply discarded.

This point of theatrical history has a bearing upon how one should approach the texts of such plays as the Digby *Mary Magdalene* and *The Conversion of St. Paul*, which come from a manuscript whose "three and a half plays are themselves in a variety of hands," of which six can be confidently identified besides "the various bits of writing that occur here and there throughout the leaves, particularly in the *Children*, where a later hand has made numerous additions and revisions."[22] One should regard revisions as normal in the register of the York cycle, or in the manuscripts which underlie the surviving Chester MSS. As the Chester editors point out:

> The assumption of a fixed cycle form seems to underlie editorial and critical discussions, but it is one that for Chester at least, we find misleading.[23]

But revisions should *a priori* be approached in these saint plays as evidence of revamping for alternative and quite separate performances, unless compelling evidence becomes available to the contrary.

III

The place and manner of performance of medieval drama is a subject about which there once abounded a great deal of misinformation – one recalls for example the off-hand remarks of F.J. Furnivall which I quoted earlier. Patient investigation of records has allowed us to correct much; the lively debate over processional productions at York, Chester and Wakefield is a recent example. I began by claiming the importance of a knowledge of the place and manner of performance of a text, using Shakespeare as my example. Most modern readers of Elizabethan plays are aware of Elizabethan stage arrangements – among other things, editors have repeatedly acquainted their readers with an outline of the evidence. It is generally agreed that readers and directors need to understand the nature of the "theatre" which was envisaged for a text by its author. This need is, if anything, even more acute for medieval plays, especially those single plays which fall into a category once thought of as anomalous; we remember that Hardin Craig entitled his chapter on them "Single Mystery Plays and Parts of Cycles", implying that cycle drama was the norm and suggesting that these other plays came from smaller towns and cities where they developed slowly from liturgical roots.[24] We now realize that processional cycles are outnumbered in a census of early play-records, and that stationary plays were more widespread although they developed in many cases later and their existence was more fleeting than the established civic cycles. Editors of independent civic plays need carefully to sift all the new evidence which is becoming available, and to include in their introductions, notes, and editorial stage-directions an account of the nature of their texts as staged dramas.

Evidence about playing places survives, of course, within the texts themselves, but it is often scanty and open to various interpretations. A character may mention the theatrical space, but not with the aim of archaeological exactness. We begin with the frequent directions in plays and interludes which mention the "place"; Dux Moraud, for example, commands obedience:

> I prey ʒow, lordyngys so hende,
> No yangelyngys ʒe mak in þis folde
> Today;
> Als ʒe are louely in fas,
> Set ʒow alle semly in plas[25]

Often the physical conditions of the theatre may be mingled with the setting of the play's action, as in the "sea" episode of the Digby *Mary Magdalene:*

> [Regina] A! Lady! helpp in þis nede,
> þat In þis flod we drench natt.
> (ll 1746–7)

Here I include the lines from *A Midsummer Night's Dream* which supply my title. Stage-directions may also refer to the imaginative setting rather than the theatre space, such as Mary's direction later in *Mary Magdalene*, "Her goth mary In-to þe wyldernesse..." (l 1972). The interpretation of such directions is our task; rather than putting the evidence aside with the belief that "make-believe will do wonders," we begin by noticing that its cumulative impression is one of dramatists who wrote with a clear idea of the possibilities and limitations of the theatrical spaces for which they were writing. The external evidence about fixed playing places is often fleeting allusions in payment records; such notices are found in all parts of Britain. This is not the place for a complete census, but let me mention a few allusions: the church hay or the belhay (Bodmin and Kendal respectively), the little park (used at sundry times for two plays, and in 1466 for a rehearsal of the Smiths' pageant at Coventry), a field (Bassingbourn), the market cross, "markit-stede", or "foro civitatis" (Kilkenny, Louth, and Carlisle respectively), the street (Kendal and Lydd), the churchyard (Bungay and Shrewsbury), the "pightell" (Chelmsford), the game place (Walsham-le-Willows and Great Yarmouth), and the abbey and the quarry (Shrewsbury). The evidence can give an impression of perfunctoriness, making do, or improvisation – the sort of impression which Shakespeare presents for comic effect with the mechanicals' rehearsal and play in *A Midsummer Night's Dream*. After all, who would put on a play in a "pightell"? or on a green? or in a quarry? Or, one might add, with a hawthorn-brake for a tiring house, even at a rehearsal? How do we find out moonshine? The impression of amateur improvisation is conveyed in some modern discussions of staging. Glynne Wickham, for example, notes that there are many more indications of fixed stages than processional ones in England, but when he writes about the staging of saint plays he notes an association "in the records of plays performed in the summer months with fields, and ... in the winter months with churches."[26]

Fragmentary details about playing places survive from only a few localities, and many of the records have only recently come to light. They suggest that the impression of crudeness or artlessness is false. The arrangements at Bodmin, Clerkenwell fields, or in the game places and churchyards of East Anglia strike one as careful and well-planned. The Bungay accounts give details about the preparation of the churchyard, the borrowing of costumes and other gear (from, among other people, my lord of Surrey), the erecting of booths and a scaffold, and so on. At Shrewsbury the bailiffs and aldermen supplied large sums for civic religious drama in the sixteenth century, and they mention the dismantling of a "frame of timber" and its removal from the theatre space in 1575. Their productions were lavish enough to include the riding of the three Kings of Cologne, and the inclusion, in a 1492–3 performance, of the King's lion. While we must not assume that lavish finances are equatable with art, we can at least escape the assumption that medieval productions exhibited neither.

In fact, the surviving texts for stationary presentation make tremendous demands upon the producer – they are "big" theatre. Probably the best-known such text is *The Castle of Perseverance*, whose remarkable stage-plan has had a great influence upon our notions about fixed stages. It requires a massive circular place about a hundred and twenty feet in diameter, a central castle structure, and five scaffolds – these details are familiar from the University of Toronto production in 1979, and from Richard Southern's widely influential book, *The Medieval Theatre in the Round* (1957). Most now do not agree with his conclusion that a vast moat and embankment surrounded the place, but at least the tremendous scope of this production is evident. The plan for the Cornish *Buenans Meriasek* also survives, and indicates the scaffold arrangements to be used over two days.

Professor Southern's book has been influential in a way perhaps unforeseen by its author. Increasingly since its publication, scholars have tended to conceive of all stationary productions as using a place-and-scaffold arrangement, with the audience arranged around the place. Also, as A.C. Cawley has pointed out, Southern's ideas came to seem sensible to investigators who pondered the difficulties of processional staging; hence production in the round was advanced as the real method for York, Chester and Wakefield, and it seemed for a time as if "round" staging was going to engulf all medieval theatre.[27] Virtually no details of other stationary theatre spaces have been available, and so in interpreting the actions of outdoor plays *The Castle* plan has become normative. Its preservation in the text of the play, on the other hand, could result from its singularity; it might be that it represents an unusual staging method, particularly for a travelling play, and hence a diagram was thought necessary to instruct the producers. It is worth noting that the only unmistakable "place" associated with a round plan is in Cornwall, where the pre-existent features of the ground could be used. As in all cases where one generalizes from scanty evidence, the danger lurks that we have inferred a "playing style" too easily.

As a result of my research at Shrewsbury, I can now confidently assert that "round" theatre spaces were not the only possibility available. In turn, this fact alters the task of the editor in approaching the text, notes, and introduction of an edition. There is not time here to go into details, but the quarry theatre at Shrewsbury provides evidence for another type of stationary playing place. As did Professor Arthur Freeman before me,[28] I began by assuming that the quarry was a theatre in the round, used on a number of recorded occasions for civic plays between 1445–6 and 1570. When I began my research into the records, the details in the bailiffs' financial accounts certainly did not contradict the assumption, and I envisaged place-and-scaffold arrangements in the style with which Richard Southern has made us familiar. The bailiffs' accounts record lump-sum payments for plays, one or two lists of props or breakdowns of payments, and a few play-titles, indicating mainly folk plays and saint plays.

Beyond the financial records, however, there are preserved documents from two lawsuits over control of the land in which the quarry was situated, a box of deeds to properties within those lands, and various maps and plans from the late seventeenth to the late nineteenth centuries. Piecing all these together produces a picture of a different shape than circular; as at Cornwall, the Shrewsbury producers used a pre-existing geographical feature, the "dry quarry" – a shallow semi-circular amphitheatre excavated into the side of a slope about eight metres high. On the sloping sides of the excavations, stepped seats appear to have been hewn at some time out of the stone and clay (these were still visible in 1779). The Quarry was used as a game place as well as a theatre – mention is made of running, wrestling, leaping, silver game playing, and the like, and it was used at least once for the performance of travelling bears; in short, it was the normal venue for outdoor entertainments in Shrewsbury, most of which have escaped notice in the town's financial records. The appearance of the quarry must have changed over the years, because it continued to be used as a quarry after it had begun periodically to be used as a theatre. However, in the latter part of the sixteenth century its appearance suggested a Roman or Greek theatre to the poet Thomas Churchyard, who described it as being "in goodly ancient guise" in his poem *The Worthiness of Wales* (1587). We have here, I think, clear evidence of another theatre shape to place beside the two occurrences of the medieval theatre in the round; and we can be free of the "tyranny of circles" – of thinking that a stationary play must have been mounted in the round.

Turning briefly to plays staged indoors, particularly by troupes of interluders, another of Richard Southern's studies, *The Staging of Plays Before Shakespeare*, has had a similarly widespread influence. Commentators have found his conclusions attractive, and now tend to think of indoor torchlit performance in a great hall as being the normal mode of performance of an interlude. While generally this is a safe conclusion, we must keep in mind that there are almost as many records of performances in churches as there are in town halls or guild halls (sixteen, as opposed to twenty-two records), as Professor John Wasson has pointed out.[29] As with "round" outdoor staging, an editor needs to have available as wide an array of evidence as possible about different performance places, to avoid the danger of generalizing too hastily.

It is unlikely, at this juncture, that incontrovertible evidence for staging, or about the manuscript of a particular play will turn up during the REED research, just as nobody seriously expects to find *Love's Labour's Won* in a remote muniment room. Times have changed, and the field has been better tilled since Halliwell-Phillipps set out on his twenty-year quest through town records, hoping for "some trace of the poet himself". But at least, as this paper has tried to show, those who sift through records from places where no texts survive may be confident that their findings will help to ease the textual editor's task, and refine and improve his or her results.

NOTES

1. Anne Hudson, "Middle English," *Editing Medieval Texts*, ed. A.G. Rigg, New York, 1977, p 50.
2. Letter to J.O. Halliwell-Phillipps, 2 July, 1866, preserved in Halliwell-Phillipps's collection of correspondence in the Edinburgh University Library, Vol. 111, letter no. 32.
3. K.S. Block, ed., *Ludus Coventriae or the Plaie Called Corpus Christi*, EETS ES 20, London, 1922, rpt. 1960, p lvi.
4. F.J. Furnivall, ed., *The Digby Plays*, EETS ES 70, London, 1896, rpt. 1967, p xi.
5. Ian Lancashire, "Medieval Drama," *Editing Medieval Texts*, ed. A.G. Rigg, New York, 1977, pp 58–66.
6. R.W. Ingram, "To Find the Players and All That Longeth Thereto: Notes on the Production of Medieval Drama at Coventry," *The Elizabethan Theatre, V*, ed. G.R. Hibbard, Toronto, 1975, pp 25–8; Hardin Craig, ed., *Two Coventry Corpus Christi Plays*, EETS ES 87, Second Edition, London, 1957, p xvii, note 11.
7. See REED: *York*, and REED: *Coventry*, passim.
8. *The York Plays*, ed. Richard Beadle, London, 1983, Appendix 1, p 465: "The Music of Play XLV," ed. John Stevens.
9. Martin Stevens, "The Manuscript of the Towneley Plays: Its History and Editions," *PBSA*, 67 (1973), pp 231–44.
10. Malone Society Studies, London, 1935.
11. "The Digby Plays and the Chelmsford Records," *RORD*, 18 (1975), pp 103–21.
12. *The N-town Plays: a Facsimile of British Library MS Cotton Vespasian D VIII*, edited by Peter Meredith and Stanley J. Kahrl, *Leeds Texts and Monographs*, Medieval Drama Facsimile Series, IV, 1977.
13. The former example comes from a Norwich record to 1540, and the latter from the Smiths' records at Coventry, REED: *Coventry*, ed. R.W. Ingram, Toronto, 1981.

14. Malone Society *Collections*, XI (1980/1), p 146.
15. Ingram, "To Find," p 18.
16. Glynne Wickham, "The Staging of Saint Plays in England," *The Medieval Drama*, ed. Sandro Sticca, Albany, New York, 1972, pp 115–6. Cf. p 117: "they had discovered conventions of stage-craft through which to reduce the requirements of a narrative that ranged the frontiers of the known world to dimensions that could readily be provided by their fellow men in market-place, church, field, or arena."
17. Or at least, as D.F. MacKenzie reminded us in "Printers of the Mind," SB, 22 (1969), such investigations *should* be based upon a thorough historical understanding.
18. David Bevington, *From 'Mankind' to Marlowe*, Cambridge: Harvard University Press, 1962. Cf. Alfred Harbage, *Annals of English Drama*, rev. Samuel Schoenbaum, London, 1964.
19. Lancashire, pp 66–9.
20. REED: *York*, ed. A.F. Johnston and Margaret Rogerson, Toronto, 1978, p 49.
21. *Records of Plays and Players in Kent, 1450–1642*, ed. Giles Dawson, Malone Society *Collections*, VII, London, 1965, p 188.
22. Donald C. Baker and J.L. Murphy, "The Bodleian MS *E Mus.* 160 *Burial* and *Resurrection* and the Digby Plays," RES, NS 19 (1968), pp 290–93. See also their "The Late Medieval Plays of MS. Digby 133: Scribes, Dates, and Early History," RORD, 10 (1967), pp 153–66.
23. R.M. Lumiansky and David Mills, *The Chester Mystery Cycle: Essays and Documents*, Chapel Hill, 1983, pp 85–6.
24. Hardin Craig, *English Religious Drama*, Oxford, 1955, p 311.
25. *Non-cycle Plays and Fragments*, ed. Norman Davis, EETS SS 1, London, 1970, p 106.
26. Wickham, p 103.

27. "Pageant Wagon Versus Juggernaut Car," *RORD*, 13–14 (1970–71), pp 204–7.
28. Arthur Freeman, "A Round, Outside Cornwall," *Theatre Notebook*, 16 (1961), pp 10–11.
29. John Wasson, "Professional Actors in the Middle Ages and Early Renaissance," *Medieval and Renaissance Theatre in England*, I, ed. J. Leeds Barroll III and Paul Werstine, New York, 1984.

The *York Cycle* and the *Chester Cycle*: What do the records tell us?

Alexandra F. Johnston

Thirty years ago, the received understanding of the English mystery cycles was radically different. The facts were well known and established. The *York Cycle* was fully developed in 1376, its unique manuscript text dated from about 1420. The *Chester Cycle*, although its five complete manuscripts were lamentably dated after 1590, was nevertheless the oldest of the cycles, dating from 1325. Both cycles were known to have been performed from pageant wagons on the streets of the two northern cities. What scholarship had been done on the cycles was, by 1953, largely bibliographical or concerned with sources and analogues. Although Father Gardiner had recently asserted that the plays were suppressed by the Protestant authorities,[1] the view that they came to an end because of the poverty and disinterest of their producers was generally held. Little criticism existed and, what did, tended to equate an episode in *York* with the episode on the same theme in *Chester*. Nor was there much said about the production of this drama, since the revival of the truncated version of *York* for the Festival of Britain in 1950 had been only three years earlier. English medieval Biblical drama as represented by these two civic cycles was a known quantity – known and considered by all but a few dedicated scholars as dull and unprofitable.

It has always given me much pleasure that the man who began the revolution in our understanding of medieval drama was a Canadian, Professor F.M. Salter of the University of Alberta, and that his bombshell was thrown at the University of Toronto in the Alexander Lectures of 1954. One of the great ironies of those lectures was that the audience, who, I have since been told, both enjoyed the lectures and were intrigued by them, had no understanding of the fundamental significance for the field of Salter's conclusions. He remarks rather endearingly at the end of the first lecture that had sketched in the history of medieval drama, "At this point, I conclude the reading of the first lesson. No great addition has been made in it to previous knowledge of English drama in the Middle Ages, but I have been fighting Homeric battles in the Notes!"[2]

What Salter did in those lectures was to reassess radically the external evidence (that is the evidence from the records) concerning the *Chester Cycle*. He banished forever the myths of Sir John Arneway, mayor and original patron of the plays, of the authorship of Ranulph Higden and of the date of 1325. He also set the plays in their proper place within the context of the city of Chester emphasizing the lavishness of the productions and the centrality of the guilds who produced them in the economic life of the city. For me and perhaps for many of us, to read Salter's easy prose was to be caught up in his enthusiasm for his subject. He was a breath of fresh air in the dusty atmosphere of early drama scholarship.

Since 1954 and more particularly in the last decade, there has been an explosion in scholarship on the two cycle plays.

The dramatic records of both cities have been edited and published through Records of Early English Drama[3], new editions of both cycles have appeared[4] and facsimiles of the York manuscript and two of the five Chester manuscripts have been made available.[5] As a by-product of these major editorial undertakings, there has been a spate of articles by the editor of the Chester records, L.M. Clopper,[6] the editors of the York records, myself and Margaret Rogerson[7], the editor of the new Arnold *York* edition, Richard Beadle and his co-editor of the York facsimile, Peter Meredith.[8] R.M. Lumiansky and David Mills, the editors of the new Early English Text Society *Chester* and the two Chester facsimiles have produced an important collection of essays in a separate volume, together with an essay on the music of the cycle by Richard Rastall.[9]

All of this activity has led us to a new understanding of the facts related to the cycles. And so, to return to my title, the first thing that the records tell us about the cycles is their real dates. It is now generally agreed that we cannot determine the nature of the *York Cycle* before about 1415 and that the date of the manuscript is between 1463 and 1477 (although I would myself argue it is closer to 1477 than 1463). In other words, the relevant dates for the *York Cycle* have been advanced by about fifty years. Our understanding of the history of the *Chester Cycle* has been more fundamentally changed. The dates of the manuscripts remain the same (all are antiquarian copies derived from an exemplar) but the date for the first performance of the text, as it has survived, has been put at 1521. In thirty years the *Chester Cycle* has become two hundred years younger than earlier scholars thought. This radical redating turns what has been considered a "medieval" play into a Tudor one.

The records also tell us the performance history of the cycles. In summary, *York* is early fifteenth century in concept, its text (or at least the largest part of its text) was committed to the manuscript we have in the third quarter of the fifteenth century. The play was performed annually except in extraordinary circumstances (such as plague, civil war or the substitution of the Creed or Pater Noster Play) until 1550. Although revived in all its splendour in the reign of Mary, the performance of the cycle during the first decade of Elizabeth's reign is spotty and the last known performance was 1569. *Chester*, on the other hand, is early sixteenth century in concept and there is hard evidence for only six performances between 1521 and the last performance in 1575.

These were the broad generalities with which I conceived this paper. At this point, it had been my intention to consider the detailed evidence that survives for two pageants in the *York Cycle* (The Last Supper and Judgment) and three pageants in the *Chester Cycle* (The Shepherds Play, the Presentation in the Temple and the Scourging) from the guild records. But as I have worked over the materials, reviewing and digesting the work of my colleagues and reconsidering my own presuppositons about these cycles, intriguing and newly-realized facts about the organization and control of these cycles as reflected in their surviving manuscripts and records, have led me in a new direction. Indeed, the third major thing that the records help us to understand is the nature of the manuscripts themselves.

The appearance in 1983 of *The Chester Mystery Cycle: Essays and Documents* by R.M. Lumiansky and David Mills is, in many ways, as important as Salter's lectures in adjusting our understanding of the nature of the *Chester Cycle*. It is the result of years of scholarship and intimate involvement with the Chester manuscripts. It also draws heavily on the work of Larry Clopper. In a paper like this one, it is impossible to rehearse the total argument that they present. When I fully understood the thrust of their discourse, I set out to track down their evidence and armed with the facsimiles and the *Chester Records*, I spent an engrossing day checking the evidence. I am convinced that they are right. Briefly, here are their conclusions:

1. The extant manuscripts are all versions of an exemplar which was itself a compendium containing within it variant versions of episodes to be chosen by the civic authorities as they saw fit for any given performance. They write, "'The Chester Cycle' is a convenient abstraction; there is no reconstructable definitive form of the cycle, but a text that perhaps from the outset incorporated a number of different possibilities and that in any case was subject to frequent revision"[10]. With characteristic understatement they conclude their discussion of the manuscripts, "What seems to us more important ... is the implication of the discussion for the concept of the 'Chester Cycle.' There were many forms of this cycle, and some of the possibilities are incorporated in our present texts, making our edition 'a cycle of cycles' rather than a definitive form. The assumption of a fixed cycle-form seems to underlie editorial discussion and also critical discussions of medieval play cycles, but it is one that, for Chester at least, we find misleading."[11] The *Chester Cycle* is, then, not an artistic unit but rather like an insurance policy with all the option clauses left in.
2. In their discussion of the manuscripts, Lumiansky and Mills make it very clear that we have the same problems with them as we have with the *Castle* manuscript.[12] Stage directions and marginal notations that probably reflect individual performance practices have been incorporated into the homogenous text along with various alternate scenes.
3. Lumiansky and Mills argue, from the evidence of the records, that the Mayor and Council bore the final responsibility for the play-texts. A note contained in the sequence of MS Harley 2150, the manuscript of the Early Banns (dated by Clopper 1539–40) reads, "Prouided Alwais that it is at the libertie and pleasure

of the mair with the counsell of his bretheryn to Alter or Assigne any of the occupacons Aboue writen [Aboue] to any play or pagent as they shall think necessary or conuenyent /".[13] This establishes the principle and the guild evidence supports it. There are frequent payments by the Smiths and Painters for copying out the parts. Lumiansky and Mills suggest that the Original was kept by the city council and, when the form of the cycle for any given year had been decided upon, the guilds went to receive their assigned parts.[14] That their parts sometimes had little to do with the guild assignments in either the early or late banns, is clear from the detailed accounts surviving from the Shoemakers. Their assignment in both sets of Banns is the Entry into Jerusalem and yet in the single detailed account they are paying for the "bakyng of godes brede" implying that their assignment that year included the Last Supper. That same account records a payment "ffor peyntyng of the geylers ffasses" and a later one records a sum for "mending the tormentors heydes".[15] These two entries indicate that the Shoemakers were performing a large part of the Passion narrative assigned in the Banns to the Bakers and the Bowers and Fletchers.

As I have worked with this material, two further points have become clear. The first is in support of the notion that the city council is central to the control of the cycle. Both sets of Banns for this play are peculiar in that they address the guilds more frequently than they address the hoped-for audience. The Banns of *The Castle* are full of cheerful hukster[-]ing telling the story with enthusiastic "hype" designed to attract a large audience.[16] The apologetic tone, particularly of the late Banns, for the *Chester Cycle* has often been remarked upon but equally unsettling is the frequent address to the guilds. Here is the verse on the Shoemaker's pageant in the late Banns:

The storye howe to Ierusalem o*u*r sauioure tooke the waye
yo*w* Coruysers that in number full menye be
W*i*th yo*u*r Ierusalem carryage shall sett oute in playe
A co*m*mendable true storye . and worthye of memorye[17]

The second point is also illustrated by the Shoemakers' verse. The lines say that the Shoemakers have the "Ierusalem carryage". If the text was flexible and undefined then the constants in the production of the *Chester Cycle* were the carriages owned by the guilds. In other words, the play cycle was conceived as a series of permanent stage tableaux with built-in stage devices physically present in the elaborate and costly carriages of the guilds. Equally permanent features of the play cycle were probably the non-verbal "turns" such as the wrestling match in the Shepherds' Play[18] and the marvellous beasts of the Magi in the Adoration Play that later found their place in the Midsummer Show.[19] The text *qua* text was subordinate to the theatrical event, being changed according to the political and religious breezes that were particularly fickle during the life of these Whitsun Plays. If this is so, then the poetic paucity of the Chester text with its line fillers and formulaic rhymes may be explained, as well as the close to uniform verse form. The permanent cycle existed in the carriages, the expected business, and in the broad outline of the Christian story.

This is in direct contrast to the *York Cycle*. The York text that has come down to us is a unique manuscript compiled from the versions of the guild plays as they existed at the time of the compilation of the collection. Richard Beadle, the editor, is confident that there was no previous "exemplar". He writes, "The extant manuscript was unlikely to have been copied from or even modelled upon a large volume of similar character and appearance ... variations in the work of the main scribe, especially near the beginning of the manuscript, suggest that the undertaking was to him new and unusual, and that he had no model from which to proceed."[20] The city council, then, ordered a master copy for its own records half way through the life of the play cycle. But the control of the texts remained where it had always been, with the guilds. After 1500, it became customary for the city clerk or his deputy to sit with the Register, as the manuscript came to be called, at the first station. The clerks, particularly John Clerke, an important figure in the sixteenth century life of the play, as Peter Meredith has shown,[21] noted modifications in the performance from the written text. The margins of the manuscript have many careful notations against passages presumably altered. The one pageant not entered at all until 1567, the Purification in the Temple, reflects a Renaissance poetic style unlike the fifteenth-century pageants that surround it. This evidence underlines a fundamental difference between *York* and *Chester*. Whatever the overarching principles of unity informing each series, the ultimate control of the texts in Chester lay with the city but in York lay with the guilds. The York council could disallow the performance of whole plays as it did in 1561 when the Marion plays were discontinued[22] or it could preside over disputes between guilds over the jurisdiction and financing of particular pageants, but it did not control the text. This fact alone explains the presence of the texts of six York pageants (somewhat revised) in the collection of plays called the *Towneley Cycle*.[23] I believe an enigmatic document of the York Mercers for 1454 records the transfer of the text of Doomsday from the Mercers to a group of playmakers in the West Riding.[24] Since each guild controlled the text of its episode, it is not surprising that many of them are poetically rich and dramatically sophisticated. The text as it was frozen in time by commital to the Register had been honed by at least fifty and more likely sixty years of annual performance. The poetic diversity of *York* should not surprise us. What continues to surprise me are the overarching patterns of imagery that echo from one episode to another. Perhaps the annual repetition of the cycle continually kept the original pattern of imagery in the minds of the adapters.

But while the language of *York* is elaborate, the stage effects seem less complex than in *Chester*. With the exception of the hoisting devices for the plays demanding ascensions,[25] the suggested mechanical devices for the second day of creation[26] and the frequent symbolic use of light,[27] *York* has few of the spectacular stage effects that are such a feature of *Chester*. There are no talking asses,[28] no reversing trees as in the Anti-Christ pageant,[29] no magic letters as in the Purification.[30] *York* is a verbal cycle not a spectacular one. Elsewhere I have argued that the language of the episodes is bound into the processional performance.[31] Whatever the *York Cycle* became by 1569, in the 1470's when the majority of the text was registered, the *York Cycle* was a vibrant series of individual pageants whose texts were independently controlled but whose collective performance experience had forged a unity of theme, image and dramatic technique. Unlike the *Chester Cycle*, the *York* text is frozen in time and, despite the indications of later revisions, presents us with only one version of the play cycle.

What then have we learned from over a decade of intensive study by many people of the play texts and records of York and Chester? I would suggest that all we can now say that they have in common is a common plot presented to them by the scriptures and a similar mode of performance – a mode of performance probably deliberately borrowed by Chester from York since the evidence of the Corpus Christi Play that predates the surviving Whitsun Play in Chester is that it was performed in a single location.[32] The play cycles were fashioned a century apart. The theological and social context of the early fifteenth century was not the theological and social context of the early sixteenth century no matter how consciously "archaic" the devisers of the Chester Whitsun Plays were. To expect the two cycles to reflect the same world is to expect the poetry of Wallace Stevens to reflect the same world as that of Matthew Arnold. We must once and for all discard any idea that the cycle episodes can be mixed and matched as if they came from the same contemporary playhoard of some hypothetical dramatic bard of the north. But even more important for a critic of the drama, the texts are not the same kinds of manuscripts. They cannot even be compared like the texts of *Anthony and Cleopatra* and *All for Love*, to discover the difference made in an interpretation of a theme caused by a century of history and changing sensibilities. One is an acting text and one is not. One represents, as far as we can tell, a close approximation of the play cycle as performed in the 1470's. The other represents, as Lumiansky and Mills have shown, a play cycle that was *never* performed but which contains within it any number of possible play texts. In the York text we have a sharply focussed snapshot; in the Chester text we have a collage whose component pictures blur into one another. Unfortunately, we have also lost the original negatives and cannot sort out one version of the collage from another with any authority. This then, among other things, is what the records tell us. They elucidate for us the complex history of the play texts. It is to these texts and the new editions of these texts that I wish to turn now.

It is a paradox of the academic world that frequently what is learned in the process of a scholarly enterprise indicates that the enterprise itself has been undertaken on unsure premises. Much has been learned by the editors of the new editions of *York* and *Chester* and this information is now available to us all. What it has done for me, however, is to render both editions less than completely useful. Both are admirable, diplomatic texts with, in the case of *Chester* and the one episode in *York* where it is applicable (Doubting Thomas) collations of variants from the other manuscripts. Richard Beadle had an easier task with *York*; as we have seen (except for Doubting Thomas) there is only one manuscript, and if he has not supplied editorial stage directions he has expunged the anachronistic directions supplied by the first editor, Lucy Toulmin

Smith as well as her marginal notes that often misled the unwary student.[33] Lumiansky and Mills have provided us with a text based on the Huntington manuscript with two significant additons. They write, "... we concluded that we could present the *whole* of the Cycle, as it has come down to us, most conveniently for the reader by using Hm [Huntington 2] as base text with Play 1 in full from R [Harley 2013] and with H's [Harley 2124] large differences – as well as the variants in the ending of XVIII in R – included as an Appendix. In addition, the three non-cyclic manuscripts could be presented in full in a second Appendix. Such a presentation, which we have adopted, most successfully avoids the taxing complexity resulting from lengthy important differences appearing in Variant Readings and it most fairly presents the two versions of the Cycle – that of the Group and that of H."[34] Lumiansky and Mills have presented us with a monumental piece of scholarship and one that, now the companion volume of essays, the records and the two facsimiles are available, puts into our hands all that is knowable about the *Chester Cycle*. I am delighted for myself. But is this text, indeed is the *York* text, going to be useful to my graduate students coming to a thirteen-week seminar on the cycles with no previous knowledge of the subject? Indeed will they be useful to interested colleagues without background in the specific field? I am afraid not. The *York* text is better for the purpose than the *Chester* text but that is simply because, as we have seen, it is a coherent single text to which critical questions can be addressed. But can we ask critical questions of *Chester* when we do not have a single authoritative version? In the *Chester* edition we are faced with the conundrum of an impeccable job of editing in the best medieval style that has produced a drama text that cannot be studied as drama with a class, without taking a complex series of informed decisions (or educated guesses) about a possible single version.

Having reached this point in the paper, I decided to seek

the advice of Renaissance drama editors, falling back on the well-known advice to graduate students in Shakespeare, "When in doubt consult Fredson Bowers". Bowers, of course, is not dealing with a manuscript tradition but he did struggle with the problem of producing a critical text. In his talk, "Editing of Early Dramatic Texts" that was part of the Sandars Lectures in 1957–58, he addressed the issue invoking first the great name of W.W. Greg:

> Sir Walter Greg remarks that a critical edition is a "critic's edition" in opposition to a popular reading edition. Clearly, he intends to distinguish an edition that will provide a complete, correct, and accurate textual basis for critical inquiry. We may be sure that to some degree no facsimile or reprint of any single most authoritative document (or parallel text of multiple substantive documents) fulfils these conditions. To require a literary critic to solve all the complex textual problems involved in the press-variant formes of Dekkers' *Match me in London*, for instance, before he can feel safe in quoting any part of the text in a study of the play's merits is as ridiculous as it would be to insist that a literary critic should accept *in toto* either the Folio or the Second Quarto text of Hamlet and, if he revolted, to force him to decide from parallel texts, the relationship and the authority of every variant reading before he dared to quote a speech in support of character analysis.[35]

What an uncomfortable passage! – because the Lumiansky and Mills text demands just such textual decisions of its readers and does so, as we have seen, deliberately. They, like most of us, are good medievalists, preparing a text for one of the most conservative series in the world. The assumptions of Renaissance drama editing are simply not the assumptions of the editors of medieval drama. Richard Beadle comes closer to a "Renaissance" text in his new edition. Although much of his energies have been devoted to "numerous problems of a textual and bibliographical nature",[36] he has, nevertheless, presented us with a working text that is not a diplomatic reproduction of the manuscript. Emendations have been made and variants from other editions are provided at the bottom of the page. Only one of the two versions of the Cardmarkers' play is printed. The Purification play has been returned to its proper place in the sequence and the fulsome fragment of another version of the Coronation of the Virgin has been moved from its manuscript position at the end to follow the complete version of the play. He has also tackled the complex problem of the texts of the Magi play. Nevertheless, this is not the fully annotated text that Mr. Beadle hoped to produce. It does, however, unlike the Lumiansky and Mills text, fulfill the criteria that Bowers establishes for a critical text. He writes:

> A text suitable for a critic must, inevitably, be an established text. Hence, an edition is critical in the second sense that critical principles have been applied to the textual raw material of the authoritative preserved documents in order to approach as nearly as may be to the ideal of authorial fair copy by whatever necessary process of recovery, independent emendation or conflation of authorities. Such a critical edition is certainly a reading edition in that a critic need not interrupt his study of the significance of the edited text in order to solve for himself problems of its authenticity in substance or in form.[37]

What the Beadle text does not do is attempt to reconstruct what Bowers calls "the original purity of the most authoritative preserved forms of [the] author's words".[38] And here, as in much of the discussion above, it is clear that the criteria for an edition of a Renaissance dramatic text and the play cycles we have been considering cannot be the same. The oracle has been consulted but the words of the oracle do not apply. Consider, for example, how an editor of the *York Cycle* might try to establish the "the original purity ... of [the] author's words". We have, after all, the *Ordo Paginarum*, the great descriptive list of the York pageants that dates from 1415.[39] Why should not an editor take that list and the existing text committed to our manuscript sixty years later and present just those parts of the text that are represented in the *Ordo*? I submit that such a procedure would produce a text of no validity whatsoever. Consider what would happen if an editor having only Nahum Tate's version of *King Lear*[40] set out to reconstruct the "original" on the basis of the title page and cast of characters from the Pied Bull Quarto.[41] This is the kind of evidence someone attempting to recreate the 1415 cycle would be forced to use. We would know, first of all, that in the original play Lear died since the title page of the Quarto tells us so, but we would know nothing of the manner of his death. Furthermore, just as in the *Ordo*, we would find characters named who have no place in the extant text. There is no Fool in Tate's version but such a character merely listed in a cast of characters would give us no idea of his nature or function in Shakespeare's *Lear*. And as in major concerns so in minor ones. Edmund is not named in the Pied Bull Quarto nor is he in Tate where he remains the Bastard. That name would be irretrievable. And what would we make of the appearance of the King of France among the cast list for the earlier version of the story since we know from Tate that Cordelia marries Edgar so strangely described on the title page of the Quarto as having an "unfortunate life". Reconstruction of a text as it existed sixty years before the surviving version from the kind of evidence left to us is impossible. For the *York* text, at least, all we can do is what Beadle has done:

provide a clean, intelligent edition of the surviving manuscript.

But what about the Lumiansky and Mills text? In some cases, if you are alert to the textual notes, the alternate versions are very clear in the edition. The entire alternate version of Balaam and Balack in H is printed as an appendix. But what about situations such as the Slaughter of the Innocents pageant? In their volume of essays, they suggest that the apparent textual confusion in the contest between the women and the soldiers can be explained if lines 305–36 and 337–76 are alternate passages.[42] This is nowhere noted in the text as they publish it leaving the reader or critic – especially one unaware of the presumed nature of the text – puzzled by the apparent dramatic blundering of the playwright. Interestingly enough, the production of this play in May 1983, in Toronto, took the play and its redundancy as printed and built up tension around the "double" feint of the soldiers against the women. Many other instances of similar situations exist with the *Chester* text.

Bowers in his plea for a text where an editor has made choices qualifies his assertion by adding, "that its apparatus [should contain] all the necessary evidence about the relation of the edited text to the authoritative documents used as rawmaterial in its preparation whenever the critic may wish to assure himself of the precise readings of the documents upon which the edited text is directly based".[43] Lumiansky and Mills have followed this practice with the Balaam play. The question then is, "Should they have made choices every time a possible alternate reading was detected and relegated the alternate to an appendix?" We would certainly have a shorter text, though not a shorter volume, but would we have the real text? Editors of medieval drama do not have the wonderful confidence of such Shakespeare editors as Kenneth Muir who remarks concerning the 300 lines found in the *Lear* Quarto but not in the Folio, "A modern editor will, of course, restore these omitted lines ..."[44] On balance, I think Lumiansky and

Mills have done what is proper in their edition – I only wish they had alerted the reader to possible alternate readings in the text.

But does this get my graduate class any further forward in its use of either the Beadle text or the Lumiansky and Mills text? Unfortunately not. Each text must be supported by several other volumes of records and interpretations. Beadle, for example, does not provide the student within his edition with the full text of the *Ordo Paginarum* but only the second, summary list.[45] As the editor of the *York Records* I can only rejoice that the students will have to consult my work but as a practicing teacher aware of all those other considerations such as the cost and availability of material for student use, I am less happy. And if only Lumiansky and Mills had provided those splendid essays as the introductory material to their edition!

But here again we come face to face with that special problem in editing early drama of which David Bevington has reminded us – the size and diversity of the canon.[46] These two play cycles are immensely long. *Chester* as printed by Lumiansky and Mills without the appendices is approximately 11,074 lines long. *York* is 13,065, lines long. This must be compared to the full text of the Arden *Lear* which numbers about 3376 lines. The Lumiansky and Mills text as it stands is 624 pages, the Beadle text 537 pages. If either edition had provided the kind of apparatus that would make them truly useful to a student, they would have been unmanageable as single volumes – unmanageable both in size and in cost.

So what can we do? The problems facing us in providing texts is fundamental to our understanding of the nature of our material and the understanding we will convey to future generations of drama scholars. David Bevington has spoken of the misgivings he felt in following Quincy Adams in the creation of a mock-cycle in his anthology.[47] Certainly, what we now know about the diversity of dates, intentions and staging conventions of the English play cycles simply bears out those misgivings. Yet given the nature of the market another general text will not be commissioned for a long time. I have expressed my concerns about both the Lumiansky and Mills text and the Beadle text as teaching texts for graduate students and yet, given the nature of the market, fully annotated editions are out of the question. Or are they?

What if, together, we took a new approach to the problem. What if, together, we undertook to provide ourselves and our colleagues and students with usable editions at reasonable cost? How could this be done? I suggest we consider publishing fascicles – I put it this way because when I began worrying at possible solutions I saw in my mind the brown covers of the *Medieval Latin Word List* and the beige covers of the *Middle English Dictionary*. Another analogy is to approach each play cycle as a "collected work" and consider producing portions of that collected work in single editions. *York* divides into five (or six if we break up the Passion sequence) units – the Old Testament Sequence (2271 lines), the Nativity (2196 lines), the Ministry (1668 lines), the Passion (4112 lines) and the Post Resurrection episodes (2591 lines). *Chester* divides into four – the Old Testament (2280 lines), the Nativity (2101 lines), the Ministry and Passion (Day 2 – 3635 lines), and Resurrection to Judgment (Day 3 – 2699 lines). *Lear* is 3376 lines and such is the textual complexity of that play that the Arden text can print only about ten lines per page in order to leave room for collations and notes at the bottom of the page. The Arden *Lear* is 260 pages long. Each one of the separate segments I have suggested could be printed with all the apparatus we all would want for our students in the same number of pages. Such an apparatus would include a general statement about the cycle reproduced in each segment, followed by a detailed introduction to the segment, followed by the unmodernized text, followed by a glossary. I would hope that textual matters, thematic concerns and performance concerns would be part of the detailed introduction using both record evidence and the evidence of the experience of performance. Obviously, the same editor or team of editors would have to undertake all the segments of each cycle.

With the *York* and *Chester Cycles* available in nine reasonably priced and fully annotated segments, the teachers of medieval drama could organize their courses according to their own interests and the needs of the students. I could have my graduate classes buy all of *York* or all of *Chester*. Others could choose to use segments from each cycle for detailed and informed comparison of the two different plays. Still others, teaching introductory drama courses, could choose a single sequence as a sample of the genre. For the scheme to be successful, of course, *Towneley* and *N-Town* should be treated the same way. Lest anyone should think that this is a bizarre idea, I submit that one of the most successful and frequently used texts of medieval drama is Arthur Cawley's *Wakefield Pageants in the Towneley Cycle*[48] which is similar in form to the method of production that I am suggesting.

Over the last three decades, the study of medieval drama has come of age. It has been taken out of the dusty limbo to which it was consigned by earlier scholars. The combination of textual, historical and theatrical energy brought to bear on the texts has only served to enhance them. Those of us who have been involved in this revolution in early drama studies owe it to ourselves and to those who will come after us to find a solution to the problem of the teaching text. With the scholarly editions, the facsimiles, the records, and a growing practical experience of the plays in performance available to us we have the raw materials to hand. We must now turn our energies to solving the practical problems of forming those raw materials into texts that are accessible to the uninitiated. Bowers has argued that the duty of an editor is to remove the barriers that inhibit communication between the author and the reader. The nature of our texts is such that we cannot always remove the barriers, but we must help our students and our colleagues to learn how to cross them or what is one of the most remarkable forms of English literature will continue to languish in the prison of its own complexity.

NOTES

1. H.C. Gardiner, *Mysteries' End: An Investigation of the Last Days of the Medieval Religious Stage*, Yale, 1946.
2. F.M. Salter, *Medieval Drama in Chester*, Toronto, 1955, p 27.
3. L.M. Clopper, ed., REED: *Chester*, Toronto, 1979; A.F. Johnston and M. Rogerson eds., REED: *York*, 2 vols., Toronto, 1979.
4. R.M. Lumiansky and D. Mills, eds., *The Chester Mystery Cycle*, EETS SS 3, London, 1974; R. Beadle, *The York Plays*, London, 1982.
5. R.M. Lumiansky and D. Mills eds., *The Chester Mystery Cycle* (Bodley MS 175), *Leeds Texts and Monographs*: Medieval Drama Facsimiles I, Leeds, 1973; *The Chester Mystery Cycle* (Huntington MS 2), *Leeds Texts and Monographs*: Medieval Drama Facsimiles VI, Leeds, 1980; R. Beadle and P. Meredith, eds., *The York Plays*, *Leeds Texts and Monographs*: Medieval Drama Facsimiles VII, Leeds, 1983.
6. L.M. Clopper, "The Chester Plays: Frequency of Performance," *Theatre Survey*, 14 (1973), pp 46–58; "The History and Development of the Chester Cycle," *Modern Philology* 75 (1978), pp 219–46; "The Rogers' Descriptions of the Chester Plays," *Leeds Studies in English*, NS 7 (1973–4), pp 63–94; "Arnewaye, Higden and the origin of the Chester plays," REED *Newsletter* 8, number 2 (1983), pp 4–11.
7. M. Dorrell (Rogerson), "The Mayor of York and the Coronation Pageant," *Leeds Studies in English*, NS 5 (1971), pp 35–45; "Two Studies of the York Corpus Christi Play," *LSE*, NS 6 (1972), pp 63–111; "The Butchers', Saddlers', and Carpenters' Pageants: Misreadings of the York *Ordo*," *English Language Notes*, 13 (1975), 3–4; "The York Corpus Christi Play: Some Practical Details," *LSE*, NS 10 (1978), pp 97–106; "External Evidence for Dating the York Register," REED *Newsletter* 1, number 2 (1976), pp 4–5; with A.F. Johnston, "The Doomsday Pageant of the York Mercers, 1433," *LSE*,

NS 5 (1971), pp 29–34; "The York Mercers and their Pageant of Doomsday, 1433–1526," *LSE*, NS 6 (1972), pp 10–35. A.F. Johnston, "The Procession and Play of Corpus Christi in York after 1426," *LSE*, NS 7 (1973–4), pp 55–62; "The Plays of the Religious Guilds of York: the Creed Play and the Pater Noster Play," *Speculum*, L (1975), pp 55–90; "The Guild of Corpus Christi and the Procession of Corpus Christi in York," *Medieval Studies*, 38 (1976), pp 372–84; "Yule in York," REED *Newsletter* 1, number 1 (1976), pp 3–10; "York pageant houses: new evidence," REED *Newsletter* 7, number 2(1976), pp 24–5.

8. R. Beadle, "An Unnoticed Lacuna in the York Chandlers' Pageant," *So Meny People, Longages and Tonges: Philological Essays in Scots and Medieval English presented to Angus McIntosh*, M. Benskin and M.L. Samuels, eds., Edinburgh, 1981, pp 229–35; "The Origins of Abraham's Preamble in the York Play of *Abraham and Isaac*," *Yearbook of English Studies*, 9 (1981), pp 178–87; with P. Meredith "Further External Evidence for Dating the York Register (BL Additional MS 35290)," *LSE*, NS 9 (1980), pp 51–8. P. Meredith, "The Development of the York Mercers' Pageant Waggon," *Medieval English Theatre*, 1 (1979), pp 5–18; "The *Ordo Paginarum* and the Development of the York Tilemakers' Pageant," *LSE*, NS 11 (1980), pp 59–73; "John Clerke's Hand in the York Register," *LSE*, NS 12 (1981), pp 245–271.

9. R.M. Lumiansky and D. Mills, *The Chester Mystery Cycle: Essays and Documents*, Chapel Hill, 1983.

10. Lumiansky and Mills, *Essays*, p 4.

11. Ibid., pp 85–6.

12. For a full discusssion of this problem in *The Castle* see the paper of David Parry above, pp 33–64.

13. REED: *Chester*, p 33.

14. Lumiansky and Mills, *Essays*, pp 184–5.

15. REED: *Chester*, pp 49–50, 60.

16. M. Eccles, ed., *The Macro Plays*, EETS OS 262, London, 1969, pp 3–7.

17. REED: *Chester*, p 244.
18. Lumiansky and Mills, *The Chester Mystery Cycle*, EETS SS 3, pp 136–7.
19. REED: *Chester*, p 481.
20. Beadle, *The York Plays*, p 11.
21. Meredith, "John Clerke's Hand;" see also above, pp 87–8.
22. REED: *York*, pp 331–2.
23. G. England and A.W. Pollard, eds., *The Towneley Plays*, EETS ES 71, London, 1897.
24. REED: *York*, p 87.
25. See particularly Doomsday. See REED: *York*, p 55; also "The Doomsday Pageant of the York Mercers, 1433," by Johnston and Rogerson.
26. See J.C. Meagher, "The First Progress of Henry VII," *Renaissance Drama*, NS 1 (1968), p 53; REED: *York*, p 139.
27. See for example in the Cordwainers' Play of the Betrayal. Beadle, *York Plays*, p 241.
28. Lumiansky and Mills, *The Chester Mystery Cycle*, EETS SS 3, pp 88 and 471–2.
29. Ibid., p 411.
30. Ibid., pp 205–6.
31. A.F. Johnston, "The York Corpus Christi Play: a Dramatic Structure Based on Performance Practice," in Braet, Nowé and Tournoy eds., *The Theatre of the Middle Ages*, Leuven, 1985, pp 362–73.
32. REED: *Chester*, pp liii–liv.
33. L. Toulmin Smith, ed., *The York Plays*, Oxford, 1885.
34. Lumiansky and Mills, *The Chester Mystery Cycle*, EETS SS 3, pp xxxii–iii.
35. Fredson Bowers, *Textual and Literary Criticism*, Cambridge, 1959, pp 119–20.
36. Beadle, p 1.
37. Bowers, p 120.
38. Ibid., p 123.
39. REED: *York*, pp 17–26.
40. James Black, ed., Nahum Tate, *The History of King Lear*, Lincoln, Nebraska, c.1975.

41. W.W. Greg, ed., William Shakespeare, *King Lear 1608* (Pied Bull Quarto), Facsimile edition, Oxford, 1939.
42. Lumiansky and Mills, *Essays*, pp 19–20.
43. Bowers, p 120.
44. Kenneth Muir, ed., William Shakespeare, *King Lear*, The Arden Shakespeare, London, 1952, p xv.
45. Beadle, pp 25–6.
46. See above, pp 25–9.
47. See above, p 27.
48. Arthur Cawley, *The Wakefield Pageants in the Towneley Cycle*, Manchester, 1958.